LACEMAKING IN RI

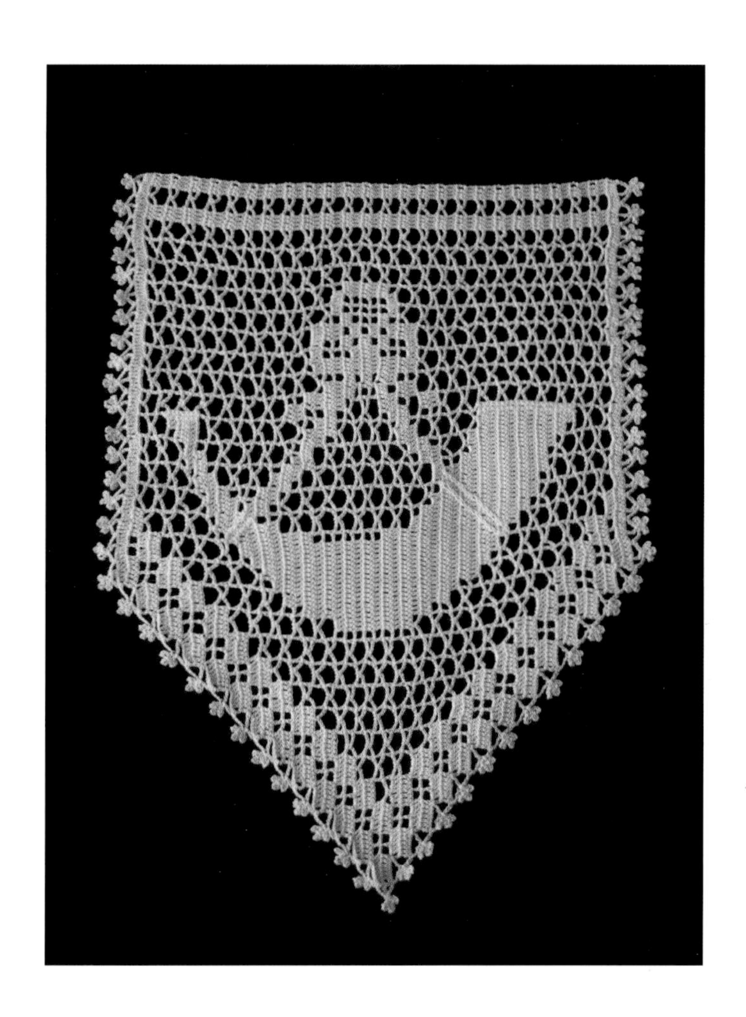

A HISTORY

Funded by

Published by
Ripon Local Studies Research Centre 2010

All patterns have been tried and tested with the materials suggested in the instructions. No liability can be accepted for any differences that may occur when using alternatives. The names of products, such as threads, are provided for information only, without infringement of copyright or trademarks.

ISBN: 978 – 0 – 9547077 – 2 – 9

Printed by

Interprint Documents Limited
Lingerfield Park, Knaresborough, North Yorkshire, HG5 9JA

ACKNOWLEDGEMENTS

We would especially like to thank the following for their help and encouragement and for allowing us to photograph some of their precious collections and to print some of their artwork.

Agence photographique de la Réunion des musées nationaux, Paris.

Carlsberg International AS.

County Publications Ltd, The Dalesman - Phil Sootheran.

County Record Office, Northallerton - Keith Sweetmore.

Jennifer Emery.

Harrogate Museums & Arts - Ros Watson.

ILSOFT Ltd

Lace Guild.

Jean Leader.

Luton Museum, Local History, Art and Archives - Dr Elizabeth Adey & Veronica Main for the artwork 'The lacemaker by the door" used in the Introduction.

Moravia DK: - Jan Novak for the artworks used in the headings for 16th, 17th & 18th Century.

National Trust, Fountains Abbey.

Parliamentary Archives, Houses of Parliament, London.

Royal Albert Museum, Exeter - Shelley Tobin & Carol McFadzean.

South Lanarkshire Council Museum Department - Gareth Hunt .

Maurice Taylor.

Warrington Borough Council Libraries, Heritage and Learning Division - Janice Hayes & Craig Sherwood.

West Yorkshire Archive Service

We would also like to thank all those who have given their help with support, advice and encouragement. No matter how great or small their contribution it has been instrumental in our achieving this book. Special thanks to Anne Marie Verbeke Billiet for her help with the Binche lace design, David Lee for proof reading, David Rivers for help and advice with fund-raising issues and Derek Edmondson for his many hours chained to an uncooperative computer.

BIBLIOGRAPHY

Brooke, M L	*Lace in the Making*	Robin & Russ Handweavers (1975)
Butterfield, M. G.	*Bishop Monkton & Environs Ancient and Modern History*	Private Publication (1958)
Channer, C. & Buck, A.	*In the Cause of English Lace*	Ruth Bean (1991)
Gott, J.	*Bits & Blots of t'owd Spot*	Crakehill Press (1987)
Hardeman, H.	*Tulekantpatronen*	Canteclear (1982)
Harrison, W.	*Ripon Millenary Record*	William Harrison (1892)
Hey, D.	*Yorkshire from AD1000*	Longman (1986)
Huetson, T. L.	*Lace and Bobbins*	David & Charles (1983)
Jourdain, M.	*Old Lace*	Batsford (1908)
Levey, S. M.	*Lace, A History*	Victoria & Albert Museum in association with W. S. Maney & Son Ltd (2004)
Lochhead, J. H.	*Lacemaking in Hamilton*	Hamilton Hardbacks (undated)
Mincoff, E. & Marriage, M.	*Pillow Lace*	Paul B. Minet (1972)
Nyrop-Larsen, J.	*Knipling efter Tegning*	Jul. Gjellerups Forlag (1955)
Palliser, B. A.	*History of Lace*	E. P. Publishing Ltd (1976)
Ripon Civic Society	*Ripon Record*	Phillimore & Co Ltd
Ritchie, C. I. A.	*Yorkshire Lace*	The Dalesman (1983)
Van der Meulen-Nulle, L. W.	*Lace*	Merlin Press (1963)
(unknown)	*Revival of Ripon Lace Industry*	Ripon Gazette (1913)
Williamson, A. J.	*Williamsons, with particular reference to Tom Williamson and his Times*	Beck & Inchbold Ltd (1931)
Winterburn, H.	*Article on Robert Aslin*	Ripon Gazette (1860)
Wright, T.	*Romance of the Lace Pillow*	H. H. Armstrong (1971)
Younge, M.	*Echoes from Ripon's Past*	Ripon Local Studies Research Centre (2004)
Younge, M.	*Ripon Market Place*	Ripon Historical Society & Ripon, Harrogate & District FHG (2001)

DEDICATION

We would like to dedicate this book to Winnie Frost (née Groves) who was born and brought up in Ripon. Her box of Lace Treasures gave us the much needed push and courage to begin our research, and at last publish this book.

Thanks also to her Granddaughter, Lyn Bidgood, who recognised the importance of the contents of her Grandmother's box, and sent them to us at the Ripon Local Studies Research Centre.

INTRODUCTION

Yon cottager, who weaves at her own door,

Pillows and bobbins all her little store;

Content though mean and cheerful if not gay,

Shuffling her threads about the livelong day,

Just earns a scanty pittance, and at night

Lies down secure, her heart and pocket light

William Cowper (1733 – 1800)

Some historians, when writing about Ripon, tell us that Ripon "once had a thriving lace industry." There have been a few articles published in the past that have explored the early beginnings of lacemaking in Ripon, but there appears to be very little evidence to substantiate what the truth might be.

Before all memory was lost of this old craft, we felt that we should bring together all the previous evidence and ideas we could find and examine them again. This we have tried to do, while putting them into context with both English and European history, with regard to both historical events and fashion, and to see how this may have affected Ripon and its lacemakers.

Authors in the past, such as Mrs. Palliser and Thomas Wright in their books about the history of lace would appear to intimate that lacemaking in Ripon was of substantial proportions. It is most probable that in Ripon, as in other parts of the country, that lacemaking was never more than a cottage industry that flourished and declined many times as demand dictated over the centuries.

With the arrival of the box of old lacemaking treasures, which we have so far traced back to Mary Johnson (née Abbott) who was born in Ripon in 1842/3, it has given us a chance to look carefully at the old bobbins, designs and prickings, and compare them to others both in this country and the continent.

The wooden bobbins resemble those still used on the continent today in both style and size. This type of bobbin was used widely in England, and is considered to be of Flemish origins. Spangled bobbins came into use in the early nineteenth century, and became very popular in some areas, including Ripon. The very early patterns for bobbin lace developed from the earlier needle lace, and seem to have been simple geometric designs. They quickly developed into more complex designs, each region developing its own style. Although this now makes each lace very different, echoes of the same early beginnings can often be seen.

Lille lace, first cited around 1582, was notable for its honeycomb ground, attractive picot headside and its bobbin made net which often incorporated intricate patterns that were highlighted by gimps. It became very popular in England and its design was copied to a great extent in the Midlands where it ultimately became known as Bucks Point. Thomas Wright tells us in his "Romance of the Lace Pillow" (1919) that during the 17th century "*At Ripon, in Yorkshire, a lace derived from Lille, and therefore bearing relationship to Bucks Point, used to be made, but the industry has long been extinct.*" Similar techniques to those used in Lille lace can clearly be seen in a few of the patterns that have been redrafted in this book, for example:

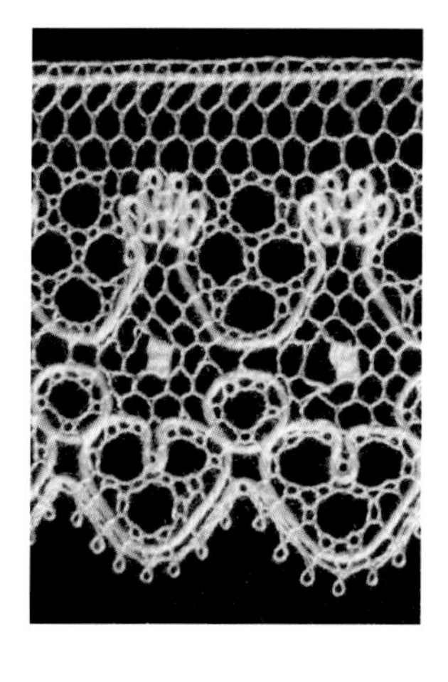

A traditional Lille design

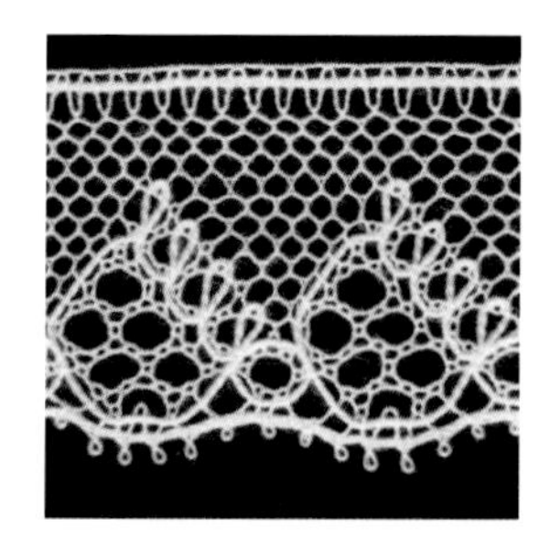

MJ11

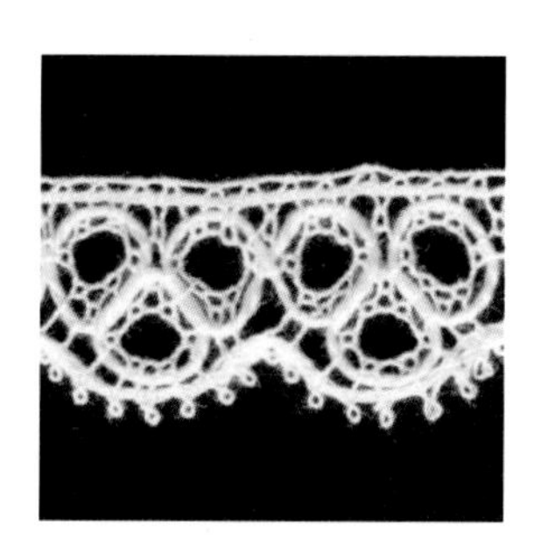

OR3

This type of lace was worked in a very fine thread and the small fruitwood un-spangled bobbins would have been quite heavy enough to maintain the necessary tension. The traditional Ripon bobbins, now very scarce, can be compared to other un-spangled lace bobbins, mostly continental, which are widely used today.

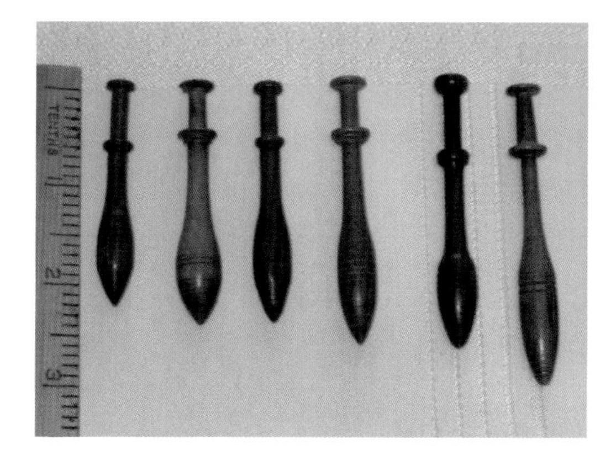

A selection of old Ripon bobbins found in Mary Johnson's box all measuring between 2 and 3 inches long.

Two old Ripon bobbins on the left lying beside a few other un-spangled, mainly Continental, lace bobbins.

16th CENTURY

The spinners and knitters in the sun,

and the free maid that weave their

threads with bones.

Twelfth Night --- *Act Two*

William Shakespeare (1564 – 1616)

Bone lace, so called because the bobbins were made from small animal bones, would seem to have developed on the continent from the middle of the sixteenth century. We do not have any definite proof of when lacemaking began in Ripon, though the fact that it is first documented early in the seventeenth century, would suggest that it could have been established for some time, possibly, even as early as the late sixteenth century. One theory has been that lacemaking in Ripon was of conventual origins. The fact that the Dissolution of the monasteries in England occurred in the first half of the sixteenth century would seem to make this unlikely.

Many lacemakers came to England at this time as refugees. The first of these arriving between 1563 and 1568 were Flemish Protestants, fleeing from the Spanish Inquisition introduced into Flanders by King Phillip the Second. Later, in 1572, following the Saint Bartholomew's Eve Massacre of French Huguenots, many more refugees arrived from France, especially the area around Lille. It is well recorded that the lacemakers among these refugees moved along the south coast west to Dorset and Devon, and north to Bedfordshire and Buckinghamshire. Because of their large numbers it would not be unreasonable to suppose that a few came further north and settled in Ripon.

Another possibility could be that some refugees arrived in Hull and travelled inland by river. At this time goods and people were carried by river as far as Ripon and even Bedale. We know that Fountains Abbey had previously had well established trade links with Flanders, France and Italy, wool and lead being transported by boat from Boroughbridge and onwards through Hull. These links would have continued to exist after the Dissolution.

Those writing about the history of Yorkshire at this time tell us that because of the poverty in rural areas the introduction of crafts was encouraged. A host of projects were introduced by the government, and new ideas brought here from abroad. These needed to be easy to set up and fit in well with rural life patterns; weaving and stocking knitting being examples of these cottage industries. In the Ripon area woollen cloth and linen were already being manufactured. Perhaps lacemaking started as part of this initiative to supplement the incomes of poor families and improve their standard of living.

By 1598 the Edict of Nantes had given the Protestants of France the freedom to practice their religion in peace and the flow of refugees ceased.

In a parliamentary report published following the 1871 census, the section which covers Yorkshire states:-

The woollen, worsted and linen manufactures have here nourished from "time immemorial", the Flemings, when they were persecuted, found a hospitable reception, and have left traces of their blood in Yorkshire.

This statement would appear to support the theories put forward in this chapter.

This illustration is an engraving of part of a larger work attributed to Martin de Vos, and dates from approximately 1585. It appears in a book on the history of Louvain published by Edward van Even in 1895.

The young girl in the foreground is working bobbin lace on the pillow on her lap, showing that this was well established in Flanders at that time. It is suggested by Thomas Wright in his book "Romance of the Lace Pillow" that the young lady behind is using a type of frame for making lace developed by the Egyptians. It could also be, by the way she is holding her threads, that she is weaving. Perhaps a small piece of tapestry for which Flanders was also famous. The representation may not be technically accurate as the work from which this was taken would have probably been allegoric in nature.

17th CENTURY

Needle pin, needle pin, stitch upon stitch,

Work the old lady out of the ditch,

If she is not out as soon as I,

A tap on the knuckles will come by and by.

A horse to carry my lady about ------

Must not look up till twenty are out.

Old lace tell sung by children as they worked

In the early years of the seventeenth century lace became very popular. Following the fashion of the King and Court it was used in great quantities by the nobility and the wealthy. Although much lace was still imported, demand would have increased greatly to supply the ordinary people, who wished to imitate those above them, but could not afford the imported lace. The local lacemakers would have prospered, as they did in all parts of the country.

It is at this time this time that we find our first references to the making of lace in Ripon. In 1629 the Mayor and Aldermen of the town petitioned the Archbishop of York to ask the King on their behalf, for permission to build a House of Correction in Ripon, so that "poor unemployed people could be taught to make bone lace and woollen cloth." This would suggest that lacemaking was sufficiently established in the town for there to be those who could teach their craft to others. Although the House of Correction was not ultimately built until 1686 we have found no evidence that these activities were instituted there.

Unknown artist

More evidence appears in the will of Alice Teasdill dated 2nd June 1635. In her will she describes herself as a "bone lacemaker". She was obviously of reasonable standing, with enough wealth to leave a number of legacies to her friends and relatives. Nothing else is known of this lady, whether she made a living from lacemaking, taught her craft to others, or acted as a dealer. No mention is made in her will of her wishes as to the distribution of her lacemaking equipment. There would seem to have been regional differences in the ups and downs of the prosperity of lacemaking. In 1626 a proposal to ban imports of foreign lace and other luxuries was introduced. This was discussed at length in the House of Lords. Lord Dorset speaking against, said that it would not be advisable to prevent imports, as other countries would retaliate by restricting our exports of lace to them, which would severely effect the twenty thousand people who relied on lacemaking for their income. This would suggest that in some regions a significant amount of lace was being exported. The Act was eventually passed but did not

Bondgate Ripon (Fossick)

reach the statute book. Ripon could have benefited from being a smaller and more isolated centre of lacemaking, and probably enjoyed a steady and continuous growth.

With the outbreak of the civil war the country was thrown into chaos, and because of this there probably began a decline in demand for lace. During the period of the commonwealth fashion for the ordinary people became much more plain, with less ornamentation of lace and embroidery. A more sober and less frivolous lifestyle was encouraged. Although the more wealthy, including Oliver Cromwell and his family did not completely give up their luxuries, lacemakers all over England, including Ripon, must have found the demand for their lace severely diminished, causing great hardship.

The return of King Charles the Second in 1660 brings with it the taste for luxury and ever more flamboyant fashions. In 1661/2 Charles issued a proclamation to enforce the Act of his father forbidding the import of foreign lace. The Act explains that it is necessary because:-
a) The people involved in the making of bone lace are unable to make a living because of imports of lace *"made in foreign parts",* and are therefore suffering great hardship.
b) The said lace and other luxuries have been entering the country without *"entering His Majesty's custom houses and paying any Duty".* His Majesty has therefore been *"deceived and defrauded".*

"La Dentellière" Johannes Vermeer (1632-1675)
photo: © RMN / Gérard Blot

The proclamation was made in November 1661 and the law came into effect that from the first of May 1662 no person was to import bone lace. The penalty, if found guilty, was £100 and forfeiture of goods. From the twenty fourth of June 1662 no foreign lace was to be sold or offered for sale, the penalty being £50 and forfeiture of goods. The fines and the impounded goods would belong to the King. It would seem that the motives of King Charles were not as altruistic as he would have had his people believe, especially as within a short period of time he issued a licence for his agent to import lace from Brussels for the use of himself and all his family.

Allhallowgate Ripon (Jim Gott)

As a result of this new law the smuggling of lace greatly increased. Those of great wealth could afford to pay the price of smuggled lace, and also to buy lace when they were travelling abroad. Those of lesser wealth, however, not wanting to be outdone in having the latest fashion, would have increased their demands on local lacemakers, Ripon included. This would have begun a new period of prosperity for those working in the lace industry.

We do not know whether lace schools existed in Ripon at this time. As mentioned earlier, we do know that the House of Correction, which would have been used for this purpose, among others, did not come into being until the end of the century.

We do have evidence from an indenture dated 1664, that a young girl named Elizabeth Doe was indentured for five years to Simon Braithwaite and his wife Issabell, to be taught the making of bone lace (see page opposite). From the parish register we find that Elizabeth, daughter of Thomas Doe and his wife Elizabeth, formerly Pickersgill, was baptised on the eighth of January 1653. She would, therefore, have been just eleven years old when her apprenticeship began at Easter of 1664. The indenture would seem to suggest that Elizabeth Doe might have been an orphan or from a very poor family. Her apprenticeship appears to have been sponsored by the overseers for the poor and the churchwardens of the town. Guidelines state the rules, which apply for the five years, and failure to comply would make the agreement null and void. The hope was that this would enable Elizabeth to keep herself in employment in the future, and not need help from the parish funds. This would mean that the lacemaking industry in Ripon was strong and thriving at this time, and was considered to be such that those involved could earn a living.

From an illustration on an Ind Coope Burton Ale beer mat – Collectors Series 12
Ind Coope is a Registered Trademark of Carlsberg International AS
(used with kind permission)

In 1685 the Edict of Nantes was revoked by the French, and the persecution of the Protestant Huguenots began once more. Again refugees fled from the horrors to both Germany and England. In England they were welcomed and helped. Those who were lacemakers brought new patterns and ideas along with their skills. We do not know if any of them eventually settled in Ripon, some names in the parish registers around this time are suggestive of foreign origins, but are not conclusive.

In 1698 William the Third improved the Act preventing the importation of foreign bone lace to make it more effective. The patronage he gave to the lace industry in this country greatly improved its prosperity. In Ripon, along with elsewhere, lace workers would have enjoyed this improvement and prospered with the expanding demand.

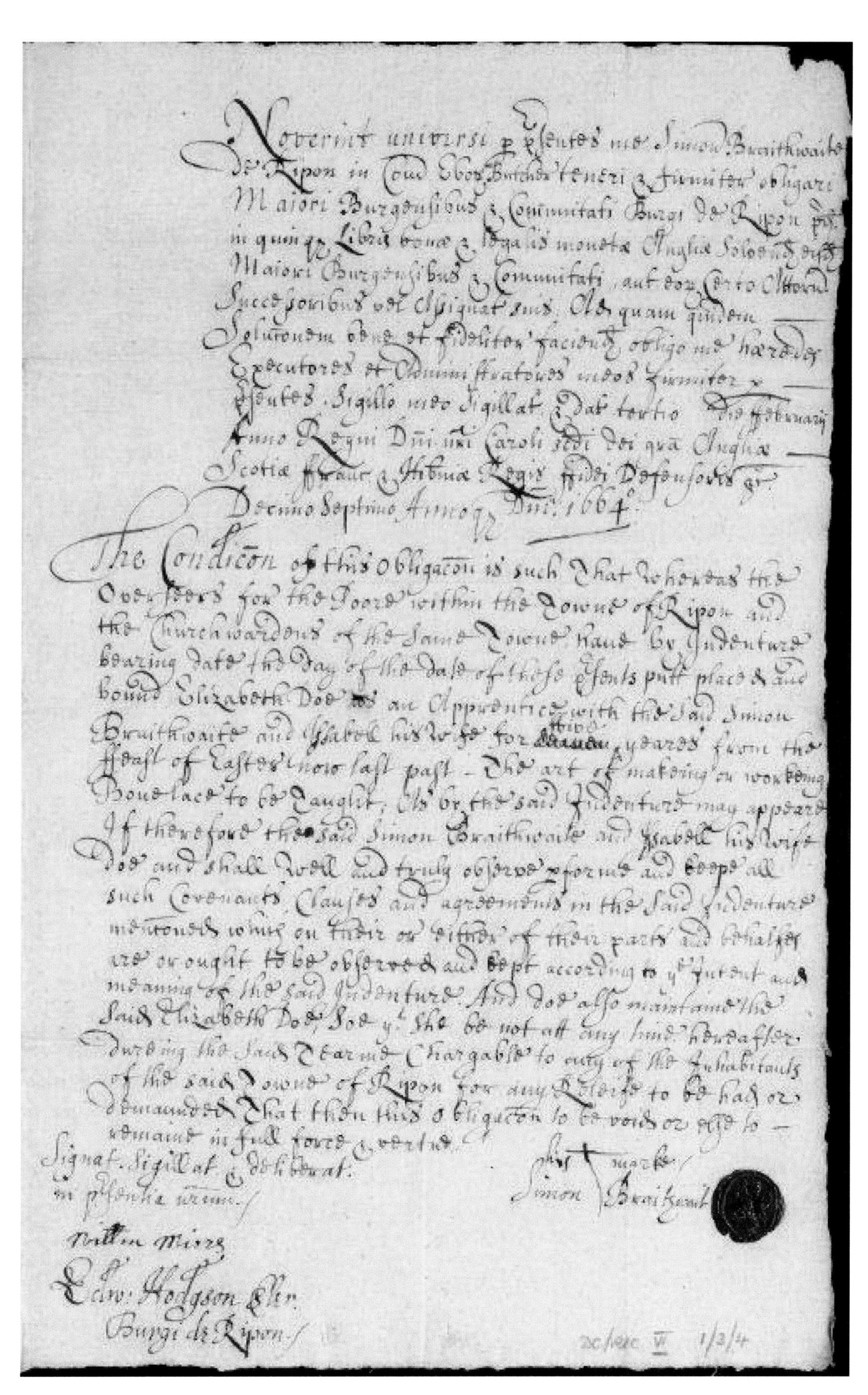

Noverint universi per presentes me Simon Braithwaite de Ripon in Com Ebor Butcher teneri & firmiter obligari Maiori Burgensibus & Communitati Burgi de Ripon predict in quinque Libris bone & legalis monete Anglie Solvend eisdem Maiori Burgensibus & Communitati, aut eor Certo Attorn Successoribus vel Assignat suis. Ad quam quidem Solutionem bene et fideliter faciend obligo me heredes Executores et Administratores meos firmiter per presentes Sigillo meo Sigillat Dat tertio die ffebruarij Anno Regni Dni nri Caroli scdi dei gra Anglie Scotie ffranc & Hibnie Regis fidei Defensoris &c Decimo septimo Annoque Dni 1664.

The Condicon of this Obligacon is such That whereas the Overseers for the Poore within the Towne of Ripon and the Churchwardens of the same Towne have by Indenture bearing date the day of the date of these presents putt place & are bound Elizabeth Doe as an Apprentice with the said Simon Braithwaite and Isabell his wife for three yeares from the ffeast of Easter now last past - The art of makeing or workeing Bonelace to be taught, As by the said Indenture may appeare If therefore the said Simon Braithwaite and Isabell his wife doe and shall well and truly observe performe and keepe all such Covenants Clauses and agreements in the said Indenture mentioned which on their or either of their parts and behalfe are or ought to be observed and kept according to ye intent and meaning of the said Indenture And doe also maintaine the said Elizabeth Doe, Soe yt she be not att any time hereafter during the said Tearme Chargeable to any of the Inhabitants of the said Towne of Ripon for any Releife to be had or demanded That then this obligacon to be void or else to remaine in full force & vertue.

Signat Sigillat & deliberat in presencia nrum

his + marke
Simon Braithwaite

Willm Mires
Edw: Hodgson Cler
Burgi de Ripon

DC/PIC VI 1/3/4

North Yorkshire County Record Office Reference DC PIC VI 1/3/4

18th CENTURY

The pattern grows, the well-depicted flower,

Wrought patiently into the snowy lawn,

Unfolds its bosom; buds and leaves and sprigs,

And curling tendrils gracefully disposed,

Follow the nimble fingers of the fair------

A wreath that cannot fade of flowers that blow

With most success when all besides decay.

William Cowper (1733—1800)

As we move into the eighteenth century little seems to immediately change. Fashions show some changes in style, but are still using rich lace trimmings, both on clothing and accessories such as ladies' fans, shoes and caps, also gentlemen's cravats which replace the lace collars more common in the previous century. The lace industry appears to remain strong and prosperous.

In 1707 Queen Anne changed the law regarding the importation of foreign lace. The Act is revoked because of objections in the Low Countries, and other places, who have been obstructing the export of wool and woollen manufactures from England in reprisal. The Act was to be repealed relating to all countries except those under the dominion of the French King. (see page opposite).

There is virtually nothing that tells us how the lacemakers in Ripon fared at this time. Writers of the time, such as Daniel Defoe and Celia Fiennes, who passed through Ripon, do not mention anything about the making of lace in the town. It is said that the ladies who made a living from making lace often lived in Bondgate and Blossomgate, the main coach routes into the town. They would sell their lace on the roadside to passengers who wished to buy; they also sold at the market or to dealers and pedlars who would sell their lace around the country.

In 1745 we see in an account from Christopher Braithwaite of Ripon to William Aislabie of Studley Royal, that there had been purchases of lace. This may well have been of local manufacture and for household use on bed linen etc. Christopher Braithwaite had his business premises on the Market Place next to the Unicorn Inn.

Anno Quinto

Annæ Reginæ.

An Act to Repeal all the Laws Prohibiting the Importation of Foreign Lace made of Thread.

hereas it is by Experience found, That an Act Passed in the Parliament holden at Westminster in the Thirteenth and Fourteenth Years of the Reign of his late Majesty King Charles the Second, Intituled, An Act Prohibiting the Importation of Foreign Bone-lace, Cut-work, Embroidery, Fringe, Band-strings, Buttons, and Needle-work, as also divers other Acts heretofore made, Prohibiting or Restraining the Importation of Foreign Lace, or for Rendring the Laws more effectual for Preventing the Importation of Foreign Lace, have Obstructed the Exportation and Vending or Selling of the Woollen Manufactures of England in the Spanish Low-Countries, and other Places Abroad: Now for the Remedy thereof, Be it Enacted, and it is hereby Enacted by the Queens most Excellent Majesty, by and with the Advice and Consent of the Lords Spiritual and Temporal, and Commons in this present Parliament Assembled, and by the Authority of the same, That the aforesaid Act of the Thirteenth and Fourteenth Years of the Reign of King Charles the Second, and also all and every other Act and Acts of Parliament whatsoever which Prohibit or Restrain the Importation, Vending or Selling of Foreign Lace, be henceforth Repealed so far forth as the said Acts relate to Foreign Lace made of Thread in the said Spanish Low-Countries, or in any other Place not within the Dominions of the French King: And that the afore-mentioned Acts, and every Clause, Matter, and Thing in them contained, so far as they relate to such Foreign Lace made of Thread (except as is before excepted) be and are hereby Repealed and made Void.

D 3 3 Provided

WILLIAM AISLABIE (1700 - 1781)

of Studley Roger, Nr. Ripon

In this portrait we can see that the fashions for gentlemen have become much less ornamented than in the previous century. The cravat is much longer and narrower, but is still made from beautiful and delicate lace. This lace would most probably have been acquired in London, local laces being of lesser quality.

Right Hon.ble Auditor Aisalabie
Bot. of Chris: Braithwaite

Date	Item	£ s d
1745 Sep.br 19th	1 3/8 yds Scarlet Cloth at 18/	1"9"3
	1 1/2 yd Scarlet Shall.n at 2"4	0"3"6
	2 Doz brest Buttons at 6d	0"1"0
	twist 5d Silk 4 1/2d thread 2d	0"0"11 1/2
	2 1/2 yds Dimothey at 14d	0"2"11
	1/2 yd fustian 6d	0"0"6
	Buck & Can.s 6d tape 1d	0"0"7
1746 Sep.br 19th	1 7/8 yd Hair Shagg at 5/	0"9"4 1/2
	3/8 Oz Silk & twist 9d thread 1d	0"0"10
Oct.r 9th	3/16 Oz Silk 4 1/2d	0"0"4 1/2
	2 1/4 yds Hair Shagg at 5/	0"11"3
No.br 10th	16 yds Green Harraleen at 17d	1"2"8
	5 1/2 yds Blew D.o at 17d	0"7"9 1/2
20th	3 1/2 yds Lace at 1 1/4d	0"0"4 1/2
	1/2 Oz thread 1d	0"0"1
Decem.r 17th	2 1/2 yds flanel at 2/	0"5"0
	thread 1d	0"0"1
Jan.ry 8th	3/16 Oz Black Silk 4 1/2d	0"0"4 1/2
Feb.ry 24th	1 Oz thread 2d 1/4 Oz Silk 6d	0"0"8
	12 yds tape 4d 1/2 yd Buck.m 6d	0"0"10
	1 Oz thread 3d	0"0"3
March 1st	1 3/8 yd Canvis at 18d	0"2"0 3/4
20th	Silk 1 1/2 1/2 Oz thread 1 1/2	0"0"3
1747 Ap. 24	5 yds Can.s at 18d 4 1/2 yds Jukil 1 1/2	0"7"8 1/2
May 8th	3 1/4 yds Can.s at 18d thread 1d	0"4"11 1/2
June 16th	1/4 yd Placn at 5"3	0"1"3 3/4
	1/2 yd Shall.n 7 1/2d 3/4 yd Dimothey 9d	0"1"4 1/2
	1 1/2 Oz thread at 2d	0"0"3
	1/4 Oz Silk 6d	0"0"6
Sep.br 15th	3/8 yd Green Cloth at 7/	0"2"6 1/2
	£	5"19"7 1/2
Nov.r	6 yds Bd Lace at 1 1/2d	0"0"9
	1/2 oz thread at 4d	0"0"2
	£	6"0"6 1/2

Rec.d Nob.r 7th 1747 ye full Contents & all Demands by Chris: Braithwaite

West Yorkshire Archive Services – Vyner MSS VR 286(B)

ELIZABETH AISLABIE

Wife of William Aislabie

In this portrait we can see that the fashion for ladies was still very much decorated, with beautiful fine lace around the neck and sleeves of the bodice of the gown. Along the edges of the overskirt a heavier lace has been used. Again the lace used for her personal attire would most likely not have been of local manufacture.

In the latter part of the century the troubles in France caused increasing numbers of refugees once again to seek safety outside their homeland, including England. We know from the Ripon Millenary that in 1775 a French refugee came to Ripon and made the acquaintance of Daniel Williamson, an artist and heraldic painter. The knowledge he brought from France played an important part in the success of the varnish works founded in Ripon by the Williamsons. They would not have been alone, as Alice J. Williamson in a book on the history of her family writes:-

> *The disruptive storm we now know as the French Revolution had the effect to missionise Europe in artistic and beautiful crafts. The fleeing refugees found refuge in England --- everywhere --- some in Ripon. Highly skilled craftsmen, guarding the secrets of their trades, were forced to sell them for a means to live.*

Some of these refugees were surely lacemakers, who brought once again new patterns, designs and skills with them to Ripon. Because of the savage destruction of Religious Houses during the reign of terror many Nuns had to flee persecution, they often had nowhere to go and were destitute. Their skills in lacemaking were a way to make a living. Some of these may have come to Ripon, being the Conventual influence referred to by Mrs. Palliser, and bringing with them the Trolly Lace designs which became popular here.

It was ultimately fashion, as always, that continued to dictate the popularity of lace, and the amounts used to decorate clothing and accessories. The use of softer materials such as muslin brought softer styles of dress, with early machine-made nets for decoration. Court Dandies such as Beau Nash in the early part of the century, and Beau Brummel in the latter, could on a whim, completely change overnight what was considered acceptable. Where they led others followed. Thus the fate of the livelihood or the lacemakers fluctuated from prosperity to poverty with some frequency. By the end of the eighteenth century lacemaking in Ripon and elsewhere was in decline.

18th Century cottages on Blossomgate. *(Jackson)*

LACEMAKER'S LAMP -----

SMALL GLOBE

Courtesy of Harrogate Museums and Arts

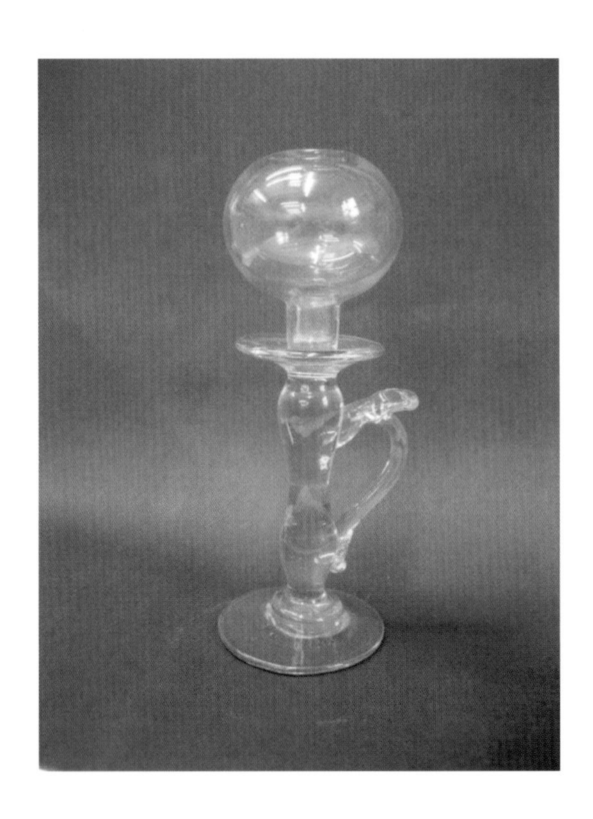

Daylight was the best for workers when making lace. Candlelight would have been the only option available in the winter months.

The small globe on the right would have been used to enhance the candlelight, and would have been for individual use. The beam of light from the candle could have been exactly directed onto the piece of lace being worked.

The globe would have been filled with the purest water available. This would have been obtained by using melted snow or ice, and possibly rain water. A stopper or cork in the top of the globe would have prevented condensation of the water inside.

By strategically placing several of these globes and candles, it would have enabled a number of lacemakers to work together in a group.

LACEMAKER'S LAMP -----

LARGE GLOBE

Courtesy of Harrogate Museums and Arts

The larger globe on the left would have been more suitable to have been used with a group of lace workers. The globes acted as a lens concentrating and whitening the light.

Those such as the ones shown here would have been made for this purpose, but some lacemakers would have had to improvise, using whatever was available to them.

FIRE POT

These pots were also known as "Dicky Pots", and were used to provide warmth for the lacemaker in cold weather.

It would not have been suitable for them to sit with their work near to an open fire of coal or wood. The smoke and dust from the fire would have contaminated their thread and lace, causing it to become dirty. This would have made their finished work unacceptable for sale at a good price.

The pot shown is made of earthenware, but they could also have been of brass or iron. The pot would have been filled with hot wood, ashes or charcoal in the morning, often obtained from the local baker, and would have continued to give warmth for most of the day.

The women would tuck the pots under their skirts against their feet. This must have been a dangerous practice as their voluminous petticoats could easily have been set alight by the hot embers. It has also been suggested that the area above the cow byre was used in winter because of it being warm, but it is difficult to imagine that this could ever have been the perfect environment.

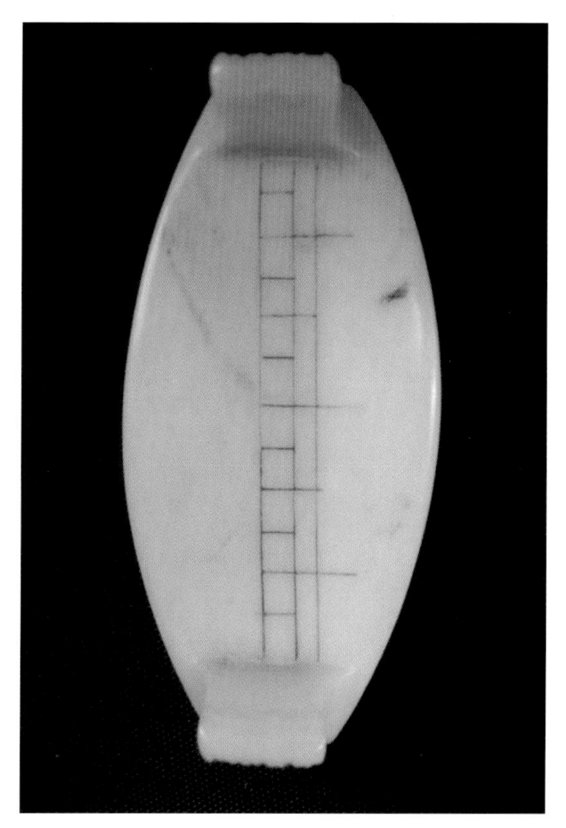

LACE MEASURE

Courtesy of Harrogate Museums and Arts

This lace measure is approximately four inches long and made of bone. The central measurement is of two full inches divided into quarters, with an extra half inch at each end.

This item seems to be unique. We have been unable to find any reference to anything similar nor have we been able to shed any light onto who it may have belonged to, or how exactly it was used.

Because of the central part of the measure being indented, it may have been used to measure the width of the lace rather than length, or of course both.

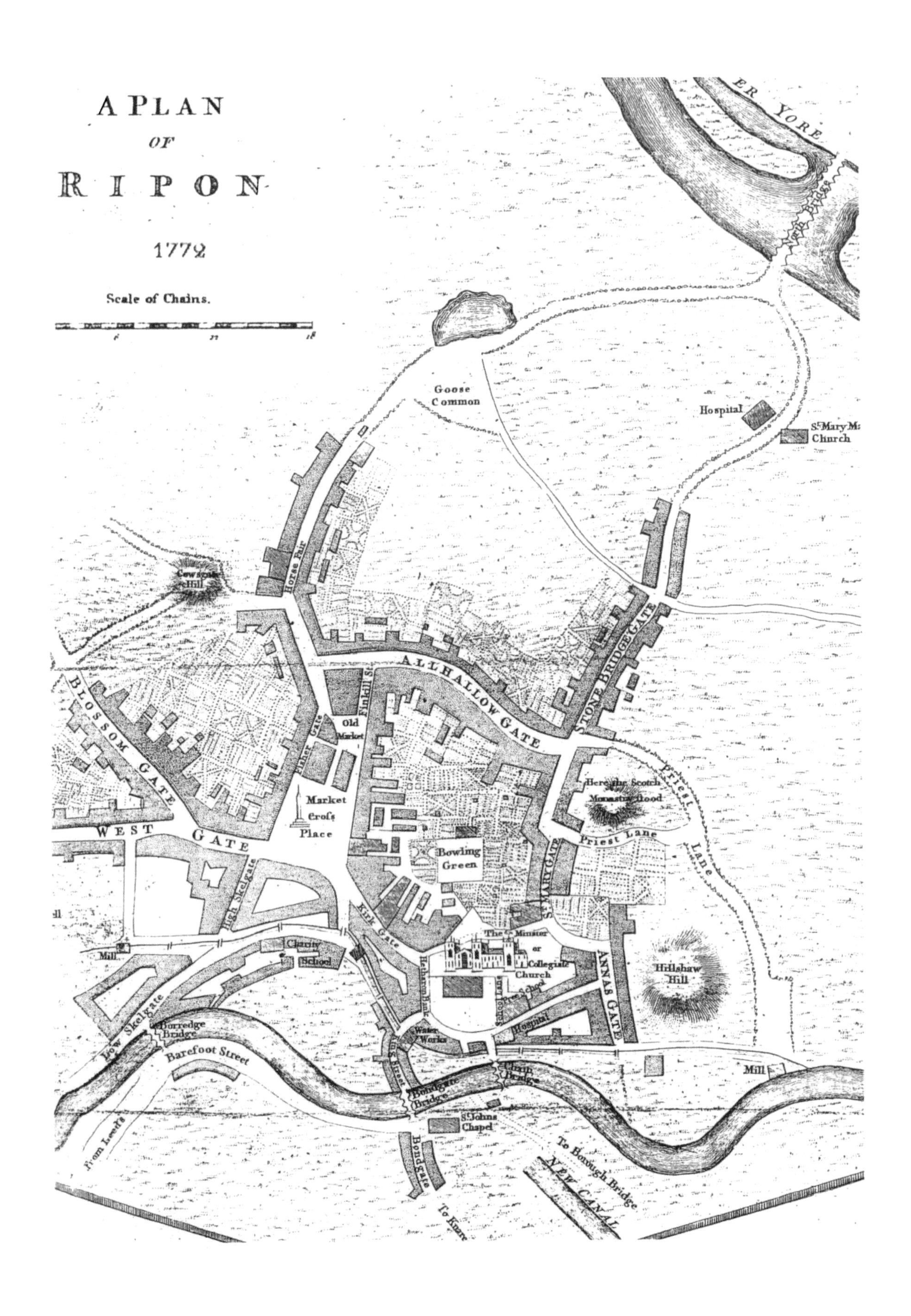
A PLAN
OF
RIPON
1772
Scale of Chains.
Goose Common
Hospital
St. Mary M. Church
Horse Fair
Allhallow Gate
Stone Bridge Gate
Blossom Gate
Old Market
Market Cross Place
West Gate
High Skelgate
Kirk Gate
Bowling Green
Priest Lane
St. Mary Gate
The Minster or Collegiate Church
Free School
Hospital
Annas Gate
Hillshaw Hill
Charity School
Mill
Low Skelgate
Borredge Bridge
Barefoot Street
Water Works
Bondgate Bridge
St. Johns Chapel
Bondgate
To Knare
To Borough Bridge
New Canal
From Leeds
Mill

MRS. LAWRENCE (1759 - 1845)

of Studley Roger, Nr. Ripon

In this portrait we see another change in fashion; the elaborate shawl like collar with intricate lace edgings, and the cap with even more delicate trimmings. It is possible that some of this lace could have been made in Ripon. Mrs. Lawrence was the granddaughter of William Aislabie, and was always much interested in the town of Ripon. She was a great benefactress of the town, and it is likely she could have supported this local industry. Some local patterns look very similar to those shown in this portrait of her.

19th CENTURY

Her work as fine as Queen Anne's Lace

That decks the country lanes in May,

Those skilled and work-worn hands embrace

Each spangled bobbin bright and gay.

So deftly joined and finely wrought,

Plait and picot, bud and bride

Flowers in thread and parchment caught,

Emblems of the countryside.

A.R. Elliott.

The early years of the nineteenth century did nothing to improve the fortunes of the lacemaker, but very slowly fashions began to change again. Ladies' gowns began once more to be embellished with ornamentation such as lace and beads. Queen Victoria, for both her Coronation and Wedding, chose to use English-made lace to decorate her gowns. This in turn caused an explosion of popularity for English lace by those wishing to imitate the new young Queen.

In Ripon we find that the 1822 Baines Directory records Richard Sheldon living in Stammergate as a lace manufacturer. In Pigot's Directory of 1834 at 16, Market Place, Alex Robson describes himself as a tea dealer and lace dealer. He was soon followed in the same property by Thomas Walker, who by 1837/8 occupies the premises as hosier and lace dealer.

Tradition implies that a man who was commonly known as "Buckinghamshire Tommy" came to Ripon in the early part of the century. He would have seem to have brought new life and enthusiasm to the declining lace industry by making prickings of new patterns, and initiating classes in lacemaking. He was said to have lived on Bedern Bank. The only person on the census returns for 1851 and 1861 fitting this description is Thomas Harrison, living on Bedern Bank and working as a barber. He came from Marston Mortaine in Bedfordshire, and was baptised on the 14th July 1793, son of Thomas Harrison and Frances Clarke. Marston Mortaine is very near the Buckinghamshire border and approximately ten miles from Olney.

Thomas married Ann Littlewood in Ripon on 9th December1823, he was described in the register as a "Hairdresser", and both were said to be of the parish of Ripon. Their children were Harriet born 1824, Mary born 1826/7, Samuel born 1831, who died at five days old, and John Prior born 1832. Thomas died aged seventy and was buried in Ripon on 11th November 1863.

Thomas Harrison brought to Ripon the Bucks Point and Torchon designs that became so popular at that period. Together with those designs brought to Ripon in the previous centuries the unique patterns to this area developed. It adds the final strand to what Mrs. Palliser describes of lacemaking in Ripon in her book on the History of Lace.

THE WARRINGTON LACE PILLOW

The lace pillow in Warrington Museum dates from around 1840 and came from Ripon. The pillow was obtained from Mrs A. Bedell, who originally came from Ripon, and it had belonged to her family. The description on the receipt at the time of purchase says that the pillow is spherical in shape, eleven and a half inches in diameter, partly covered in blue butcher's linen with white upper cloth and side pockets. Fine skein thread and brass pins. One piece of lace on parchment measures fifteen and a half inches long and four inches wide. There are one hundred and forty bobbins. The receipt is dated 21st August 1907

The pillow was exhibited during the following year and the descriptive card which accompanies the pillow in the case says: ---

LACE PILLOW

With 140 bobbins, 11 parchment patterns etc.

Ripon, Yorkshire, about 1840

The pillow and bobbins are of the pattern used in Bedfordshire and Northamptonshire. The bobbins are of bone decorated in the lathe, or of wood, inlaid with white metal or bound with brass wire. Twenty-nine of the bone bobbins bear Christian names, and five of them inscriptions indicating love gifts. Three are dated 1842, 1844. The pins and pincushion are modern, and the piece of lace on the pillow was worked by Mrs A.S.G. Bedell. 1908

THE BOBBINS

The tradition of spangled bobbins commonly used in this country today would seem to have begun in the first decade of the nineteenth century. It is unique to English bobbins, and has the effect of preventing the bobbin rolling on the pillow, and the weight of the beads helps to keep the thread hanging straight under tension. They also look cheerful and pretty. The bobbins with the Warrington Pillow are typical of those used in the early nineteenth century. Although because of deterioration of the threads over the years, it is not easy to see the bobbins individually, they are obviously very personal to the owner, and would have given great pleasure.

Old Square Cuts

THE BEADS

The beads were usually made of glass in a multitude of shapes and colours, and strung together on a circle of fine wire. They were then attached to the bottom of the bobbin. Each lacemaker would have had their own favourites. They may have come from a broken necklace, recycled because of their sentimental value, given as gifts, or bought at the local market.

Bird Cage Beads

This selection of beads with the Warrington Pillow shows the wide choice that was available.

The small square glass beads were often made by the local blacksmith. The beads were melted off one at a time from a stick of glass, the hole in the centre was made with copper wire and the sides flattened with a file. Others were imported from many places, some from the continent where Venice exported great numbers of glass beads; they also came from Africa or Syria. Many had exotic names such as Evil Eye, Serpent's Eye, Pony and even Kitty Fisher after a celebrated actress. Many other items were used as well as beads, most common were small charms or a button, even coins and shells, anything that had some special meaning.

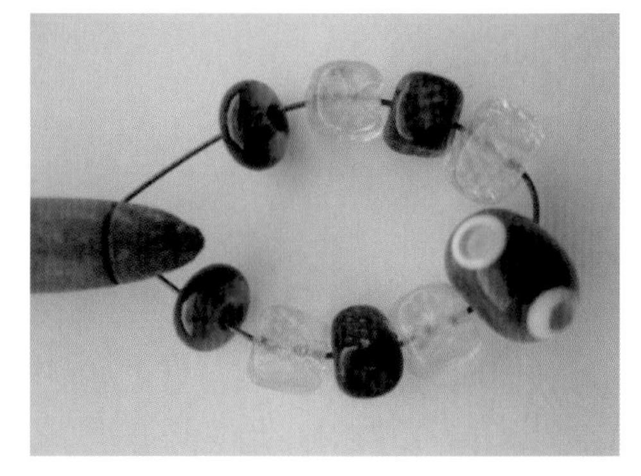

Square Cuts and Kitty Fisher's Eyes.

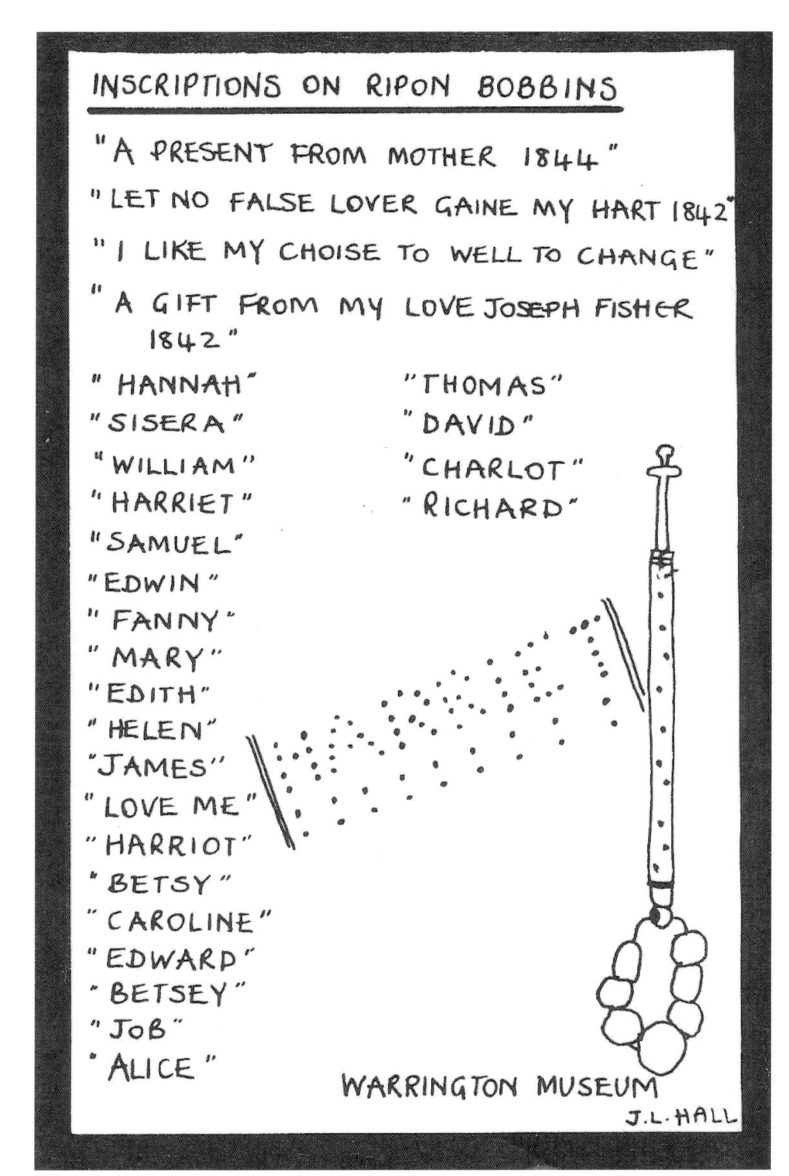

INSCRIPTIONS ON RIPON BOBBINS

"A PRESENT FROM MOTHER 1844"
"LET NO FALSE LOVER GAINE MY HART 1842"
"I LIKE MY CHOISE TO WELL TO CHANGE"
"A GIFT FROM MY LOVE JOSEPH FISHER 1842"

"HANNAH"
"SISERA"
"WILLIAM"
"HARRIET"
"SAMUEL"
"EDWIN"
"FANNY"
"MARY"
"EDITH"
"HELEN"
"JAMES"
"LOVE ME"
"HARRIOT"
"BETSY"
"CAROLINE"
"EDWARD"
"BETSEY"
"JOB"
"ALICE"
"THOMAS"
"DAVID"
"CHARLOT"
"RICHARD"

WARRINGTON MUSEUM

J.L. HALL

This is the list of the inscriptions on the bobbins of the Warrington Pillow. They seem to be mostly a collection of names of family and friends. The four with messages of affection would appear to have been given as gifts.

The list was compiled for an exhibition on lacemaking which took place in the Cathedral in 1986. This was part of a number of events that year to commemorate the hundred year anniversary of the Millenary celebrations in 1886.

For the first time in the nineteenth century we have the chance, by studying the trade directories and census returns for Ripon, to see the different trades in the town. Also where people lived, the work they did and where they came from. We can also see how things changed over time. The period of time chosen to give us this evidence for the lace industry in Ripon is the middle part of the century, and covers the years between the census of 1841 to that carried out in 1861.

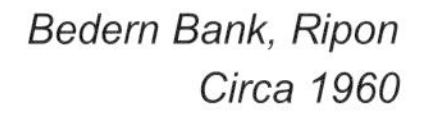

Bedern Bank, Ripon
Circa 1960

Earlier in the century the number of lace dealers had been very few, only two or three at any time, suggesting that the industry was in a period of decline. By the time we come to 1841 the trade directories show that the number was beginning to increase. This could have been because the directories were becoming more comprehensive, but the consistency of the increase in numbers makes a revival in lacemaking the more likely. Those mentioned in Pigot's Directory of 1841/2 included:--

Walker and Severs---- Market Place---- Hosiers and Lacemen, also lace manufacturers. Also Thomas Bridgewater of Middle Street, William Beckwith of Kirkgate, Thomas Binns and Elizabeth Hodgson, both of King Street. By 1848 the Market Place business has become Walker and Aslin, and the numbers have increased again to include:--

Ann Chapman of North Street, William Harper of Queen Street, Thomas Johnson of Market Place and William Abbott of Middle Street. These would have been the most substantial businesses, and there would most probably have been smaller concerns which did not warrant an entry in these directories. Two entries in the Ripon Cathedral Registers show this. Firstly, in 1837 Robert Exelby refers to himself as a lace dealer in the entry for the baptism of his son. The name of Exelby does not appear in any of the directories. Similarly, in 1839, William Harper in the entry for his daughter's baptism describes himself as a dealer in lace, but he does not appear in the directories until 1848.

Kelly's Directory of 1851 shows a fall in the number of those advertising as lace dealers, with only six names remaining. These were Walker and Aslin, Thomas Binns, Thomas and Margaret Bridgewater, Ann Chapman, William Harper and Thomas Johnson. The same directory for 1854/5 shows yet another fall in numbers, with no mention of Thomas Binns or Thomas Johnson. By 1861 only Walker and Aslin remain and advertise as General Merchants and Lace Dealers. In the picture above, the tower-like building in the top right hand corner of the Market Place was the premises of Thomas Walker.

The lace makers never appear in the trade directories, so it is through the census records that we have to search for evidence. The numbers of those who claim to make a living in this way are very few, and barely change over the period covered by the census returns for 1841, 1851 and 1861. These were:--

Ann Holdsworth	*Allhallowgate*	Phyllis Mason	*Westgate*
Sarah Ingleby	*Allhallowgate*	Elizabeth Walker	*Bondgate*
Mary Kitching	*Allhallowgate*	Jane Buckle	*Whitehouses*

Susannah Carter, Lace Weaver *High St. Agnesgate*

The fact that there would appear to be fewer people making lace than were dealing in lace would have been extremely unlikely. The explanation for this is probably that, as a cottage industry, most of the lacemakers were housewives and children supplementing the main family income, and it was not deemed necessary to enter this on the census form. Many of these workers could also have been from the surrounding villages and outlying farms. M. G. Butterfield writes in her book on Bishop Monkton, “There was once a lace industry here,” and mentions a Mrs Whitmore who made Nottingham lace. According to Mrs Palliser in her History of Lace, Nottingham lace or Run lace was made by stretching machine made net over a drum shaped frame, and a finer thread being run through the net with a needle. The pattern was followed from a drawing, and mainly seems to have been copies of Lille designs. This type of work originated in Eastern countries such as Turkey: it is impossible to say if it was widespread in the Ripon area.

With the increasing production of cheaper machine-made lace, and its growing popularity, so the demand for handmade lace declined. This time it was not fashion, but cost that influenced the change. The rise and fall in lace dealers seen over this period would have been reflected in the numbers of lace makers, with a sharp fall as demand decreased, thus leaving only a small core of traditional workers as we move towards the end of the century.

The firm founded by Thomas Walker at 16, Market Place, would appear to have been the largest and most prosperous in Ripon. He had moved his business from Middle Street into larger premises by 1837, trading as a Hosier and Lace Dealer. By 1841 he had formed a partnership with George Severs, who had been trading in the Market Place as a Linen and Woollen Draper, and also as a laceman. The partnership was short-lived, George Severs died in 1848, and Thomas Walker formed a new partnership with Robert Aslin the same year. The business seems to have been widespread, with Thomas Walker owning property in Harrogate and warehouses in Birmingham and Sheffield. In 1855 a new Warehouse was opened in Kirkgate offering “A large stock of Worsteds, Lamb’s Wool and Knitting Cottons” also Hosiery, Millinery and Lace. Following Thomas Walker’s death in 1858 Robert Aslin carried on the business, possibly with Thomas’s nephew. After the death of Thomas’s wife Sarah in 1875 Robert Aslin bought the property from the executors of Thomas Walker’s Will. Robert continued the business until his death in 1888, and between 1891 and 1897 it was purchased by John Rayner. The property was demolished in 1905.

LACE, MILLINERY, & HOSIERY WAREHOUSE,
KIRKGATE, RIPON.

T. WALKER begs most respectfully to inform the inhabitants of Ripon and its vicinity, that he has opened the Shop at the top of Kirkgate, lately occupied by Mr. Wm. Parker, Confectioner, with a large and well-selected Stock of Hosiery, Millinery, and Lace Goods, all of which will be offered at ehe very lowest prices.

An early inspection will oblige.

N.B.—A large stock of Worsteds; Lambs' Wool and Knitting Cottons, of every shade and quality, always on hand.

Ripon & Richmond Chronicle 1855

This old print of Ripon Market Place dates from circa, 1850. It is of interest as the building at the right hand corner with Kirkgate is an earlier property which had belonged to Christopher Braithwaite in the 18th century. The building at the top left hand corner is that owned by the Walker/ Severs/ Aslin business partnerships.

GEORGE SEVERS 1811 - 1848

George was baptised on June 16th 1811, the son of John Severs and his wife Ann, formerly Brigham. His father is described in the register as a carpenter. On June 10th 1837 George Severs married Elizabeth Stevenson of Gow Busk, Sawley whose family were farmers.

Pigot's Directory for 1834 notes that John and George Severs were trading as Linen and Woollen Drapers on Market Place in Ripon. White's Directory names only George as the proprietor of the business in 1837. By 1841 George Severs and Thomas Walker have merged their businesses, and are trading as Walker and Severs at 16, Market Place. They describe themselves as Hosiers, Lace Dealers and Manufacturers. The 1841 census shows that George lived on the premises of the business with his wife and their two children.

In 1848 George died aged 37 years, and was buried in the graveyard of Trinity Church. His widow Elizabeth moved to live on Coltsgate Hill with her children George, Jane, Ann and Samuel. They were supported by a private income.

ROBERT ASLIN 1816 - 1888

Robert Aslin was baptised on January 5th 1816 in Haworth, son of John Aslin, a Wesleyan Minister, and his wife Hannah, formerly Haigh. By 1825 the family had moved and were living in Bedale.

Because he was Nonconformist we have no available record of baptisms or marriages, and can rely only on other sources. The next time we find Robert Aslin is in the trade directory for 1848, when we see he has joined Thomas Walker in the business at 16, Market Place, Ripon, which has become Walker and Aslin, General Merchants and Lace Dealers. In 1850 his infant daughter and his wife Martha died in childbirth, and are buried in the graveyard of Trinity Church. The 1851 Census shows Robert as a widower living at the business premises on Market Place. In 1855 he was elected as a member of the Council, and served as a member until 1861.

In the 1861 Census Robert Aslin had moved to 25, North Street, with two young daughters. He is once more a widower following the death of his three year old daughter in 1860, also his second wife Mary in childbirth, followed by the death of his infant son early in 1861. All are buried in the graveyard of Trinity Church.

Robert Aslin was instrumental in the formation of the Ripon Volunteer Rifles. Joining on March 31st 1860 he served in various capacities until his resignation on February 16th 1873. We find his family again on the 1871 Census still living on North Street with his third wife Catherine and his children. He is described as a Draper employing four boys. Catherine died shortly after this and is buried in Penrith. In the 1881 Census Robert is still living on North Street with some of his family, once more a widower. He appears to have been considered rather eccentric, possibly because, being a keen astronomer, he had built an observatory in his garden, where he spent many hours at night studying the stars through a "Monster Telescope". In February 1888 it would appear he lost his fourth wife Emily, who was buried during that month. Robert Aslin died on May 28th 1888, and following a service at the Wesleyan Chapel he was buried in the graveyard of Trinity Church. There were a huge number of mourners at his funeral who came to pay their respects. He was described as 'a very respected citizen and a good Christian man'.

Robert Aslin's premises at 16, Market Place 1897

Old cottages on Allhallowgate Ripon

Thomas Walker and also some of the lacemakers lived on this street.

THOMAS WALKER 1792 - 1858

Thomas was baptised on December 2nd 1792, the son of Oswald Walker of Ripon and his wife. We know that he married his wife Sarah, who was born in Burnley in Lancashire, circa 1820. In the Ripon Cathedral Registers there are three entries for baptisms of children of Thomas and Sarah Walker in 1823, 1825 and 1829. In each of these Thomas is described as a Licensed Hawker, also in 1825 as Lace Dealer.

In the Pigot's Directory for 1829 his business has flourished sufficiently for him to have moved into premises in Middle Street, where he traded as a Lace Dealer. Thomas continued in these premises for a short period of time, but by 1837 he had moved to larger premises at number 16, Market place, now trading as Hosier and Lace Dealer.

The directory for 1841 shows that he had formed a partnership with George Severs, a Linen and Woollen Draper. In the same year the census also shows that Thomas and his wife Sarah were living on Allhallowgate. In 1848 George Severs died, and Thomas quickly made a new partnership with Robert Aslin the same year.

In 1854 Thomas Walker was elected to serve on the council, and continued to do so until his death in 1858. A new addition to the business was opened in 1855 on Kirkgate. He also owned property in Harrogate, and warehousing in Sheffield and Birmingham.

Thomas Walker died in 1858, and was buried in the Temple Graveyard. In his will he left a contribution of one hundred pounds for the Temperance Hall on Duck Hill. Other assets were left in trust to provide for his widow, they were then to be sold by his executors on her death.

In 1840 the Mechanics' Institute organised an exhibition of an industrial character which was a great attraction in the town. It was believed to be one of the first held in Yorkshire. On show were rare and curious articles, paintings and antiquities from the local mansions, machinery and spinning and weaving. No mention is found of the lacemaking in Ripon. This type of exhibition became very popular around the country, especially after the Great Exhibition in London in 1851. Even so, it was 1864 before the Ripon Scientific Society joined with the Mechanics' Institute to present a limited Fine Art Exhibition. This proved so popular, and attracted such a large attendance, that a larger exhibition was arranged in 1870. From the programme we can see that a large amount of lace items were included, although few would seem to have been of Ripon origin.

OFFICIAL CATALOGUE
OF
THE EXHIBITION
OF
WORKS OF ART,
Antiquities, Natural History, Curiosities,
&c., &c.,
AT RIPON,
FOR THE BENEFIT OF
THE RIPON SCIENTIFIC SOCIETY
AND
MECHANICS' INSTITUTE,
OPENED ON THE 18th DAY OF APRIL, 1870.

SECOND EDITION.

PRICE 6D.

RIPON:
A. JOHNSON & Co., PRINTERS, &c., CHRONICLE OFFICE.

425	Old English point lace.	*Miss Wood*
426	Mechlin point.	*ditto*
427	Greek lace.	*Miss Ashmore*
428	Old Brussels point.	*Miss Wood*
429	Old piece of pillow lace.	*Mrs. Bower*
430	Mechlin lace.	*ditto*
431	Point lace, (bird pattern.)	*Miss Collins*
432	Brussels point.	*ditto*
433	Piece of lace.	*Mrs. Bower*
434	Point lace.	*Miss Collins*
435	Brussels point.	*Mrs. Langdale*
436	Greek point.	*Mrs. H. Oxley*
437	Lace scarf, (made by Nuns of Palermo.)	*Mrs. Lukis*
438	Greek point lace.	*Mrs. Bower*
439	Modern Brussels lace.	*ditto*
440	Greek lace.	*Mrs. H. Oxley*
441	Point lace scarf.	*Mrs. Wood*
442	Old lace veil.	*Mrs. Bower*
443	Point lace berthe.	*ditto*
444	Venetian point.	*Mrs. Wood*
445	Very fine specimen of venetian point.	*Mrs. Rohde Hawkins*
446	Venetian point.	*Mrs. Wood*
447	Limerick lace.	*Mrs. Bower*
448	Fine lace veil.	*ditto*
449	Two pieces of point lace.	*Mrs. Paley*
450	Point lace pattern.	*Mrs. Gray*
451	Fine lace lappet.	*Mrs. Wood*
452	Curious sample of lace.	*Miss Gray*
453	Venetian guipure.	*Mrs. Langdale*
454	Mechlin lace.	*Miss Collins.*
455	Fragment of very fine old lace.	*Mrs. Rohde Hawkins*
456	Point lace	*Mrs. Bower*
457	Modern Brussels lace.	*ditto*

There were three more Industrial Exhibitions towards the end of the century. The first in 1892 and the second in 1893 were in the Victoria Hall, and seem to have been well supported. The third in 1895 was opened by the Bishop of Ripon, its object being to promote industrious habits among the working classes. It did not enjoy the same success as those before, and was not well attended.

By the end of the nineteenth century, lacemaking as a working industry has almost come to an end, with only a very few old ladies making lace to supplement their income. Although they seemed to have passed on their skills to some of the wealthier ladies of the town, who enjoyed making the lace for pleasure, industrialisation and a changing world sealed the fate of the craft of lacemaking, not only in Ripon, but the whole of the country.

Photograph Courtesy of Harrogate Museums and Arts.

No.	Item	Lent by
458	Greek lace.	*Mrs. H. Oxley*
459	Ditto	*ditto*
460	Old pillow lace.	*Mrs. Bower*
461	Piece of lace.	*Mrs. H. Oxley*
462	Ditto	*ditto*
463	Ditto	*ditto*
464	Ditto	*ditto*
465	Greek lace.	*ditto*
466	Ditto	*ditto*
467	Piece of lace.	*ditto*
468	Flounce of Palermo lace.	*Mrs. Lukis*
469	Lace of the 19th century.	*Mrs. Paley*
470	Piece of Brussels point lace.	*Mrs. Reynard*
471	Piece of point lace, (finished and unfinished.) 1760.	*Mrs. J. Greenwood*
472	Piece of lace, (unfinished) 1760.	*ditto*
473	Veil of exquisite Brussels lace.	*Mrs. Reynard*
473a	Piece of Greek lace.	*Mrs. J. Greenwood*
474	Very valuable ruffle of lace.	*Mrs. Reynard*
475	Fine old point.	*ditto*
476	Piece of fine Greek lace.	*ditto*
477	Piece of Brussels point.	*ditto*
478	Ditto	*ditto*
479	Piece of fine pillow lace.	*Mrs. Bower*

The above photograph shows a Ripon Lady making lace. We do not know her identity, or the date when the photograph was taken. It would most likely have been someone involved with the Exhibitions in Ripon either at the end of the nineteenth century, or at the very beginning of the twentieth century. The piece of lace on the pillow is typical of that period.

On the left is another page from the catalogue for the Exhibition that was held in Ripon in 1870. It shows more items of lace that were loaned for the event by various ladies of the city.

20th CENTURY

Old bobbins glow

As loving hands caress, and move from side to side,

The pattern grows,

She smiles, and looks upon her work with pride,

The old tradition,

Kept alive where once it was a duty,

Her composition,

Worked with pleasure, in friendship, creating beauty.

A.E. 2009

In the 1901 census there is no record of any person describing themselves as a lacemaker. Although those writing earlier articles on the subject claim to have been told that there was "one old lady still left making lace", it is more likely that there were a number of ladies still involved in lacemaking, but not in a commercial capacity.

By 1905 the Ripon Industrial Society had been re-organised to give more encouragement to arts and crafts. The Arts and Crafts movement seems to have been very strong in Ripon at this time, and they were keen to try and revive the old traditional crafts which were beginning to die out.

The Ripon Gazette reported in 1906 on a pageant held in Ripon from July the nineteenth to the twenty first. This was to celebrate one thousand and twenty years of civic life in Ripon. Miss Eliza Mason contributed to the report by writing:-
"Lace is an old Ripon Industry as the late pageant showed us by the old lady sat in her chair with her pillow on her knee....It is sad to learn that many old parchment designs have been lost, having been burned as rubbish, but there are a few clever and industrious people who still follow this fascinating and beautiful art, and many old patterns are still made".
This old lady mentioned in the article may be the lady with the lace pillow represented in the photograph.

Other exhibitions in 1907 and 1909 met with varying degrees of success. In 1909 there were one thousand and twenty exhibits; almost half of these were from schools, with prizes awarded in different classes. After this the Education Department would not allow competitive work to be carried out in school hours. In 1911, the Mayoress, keen to revive the making of lace in Ripon, held classes at her home "Aislabie", on Clotherholme Road.

The seventh exhibition of the Ripon Industrial Society in 1913 was held in the Victoria Opera House. The number of entries almost doubled those of the previous event in 1911. This time there were demonstrations in handloom weaving, spinning and lacemaking; other exhibits included needlework, crochet, painting and woodwork. There were also trade exhibits, lectures and concerts.

Numerous ladies were said to be desirous of the revival of lacemaking in Ripon, and fourteen were willing to undertake instruction. There were still some old pricking available at this time, which they hoped to reproduce. A Miss Rhodes, whose family had previously come from Ripon, was brought from the south of England to help, and encourage the revival. Later that year it was reported that the West Riding County Council had promised a grant towards the project, and would permit the use of a classroom at the Girls High School for the proposed classes. The classes were to be on Monday, Wednesday and Friday from 4.30pm until 6.00pm, and would cost six shillings (30p) for twenty six lessons, twelve pupils were required. At the same time, Mrs Harker of the Linen Warehouse on Kirkgate arranged private classes. Ten people applied at the cost of twelve shillings (60p) for twelve lessons. Classes for children were tuppence (1p) for a half hour lesson.

Inside the Victoria Opera House Water Skellgate

It was at this time that Mary Johnson, the original owner of the box of lace treasures, was making lace in Ripon. She would appear to have bought her requirements for this by mail order from a firm in Bedford, suggesting that it was no longer possible to obtain the necessary range of materials locally. The catalogue in her collection is dated 1910, and was posted to her in 1912. It contains a large selection of threads, bobbins, pins and a wide range of every other necessity that might be required by the lacemaker.

Mary Johnson was born in 1843, the daughter of William Abbott and his wife Elizabeth, formerly Middleton, of Skelton on Ure. William Abbott was a cabinet maker and upholsterer, and founder of a furniture store on North Street which has only recently been closed.

The 1861 census shows Mary living at home with her family on North Street, and at eighteen years of age describes her as a Stationer. She was probably working in another business owned by the family. In 1869 she married Robert Johnson, a Master Grocer, and in 1872 their daughter Mary Elizabeth was born. Although they had other children, all appear to have died in infancy.

In 1891 Mary Elizabeth Johnson married George Groves, Mary Elizabeth was a Milliner and Dressmaker, and George was a Joiner and Carpenter. In 1901 both families lived on Old Market Place, Robert and Mary Johnson at number thirteen trading as Grocers, and George and Mary Elizabeth at number twelve which traded in baby linen and fancy goods. Their three children were Gladys aged five, Winifred aged three, and Marjorie just one year old. Following the deaths of their parents, George in 1907 and Mary Elizabeth in 1909, Mary Johnson took over the care of her three young granddaughters.

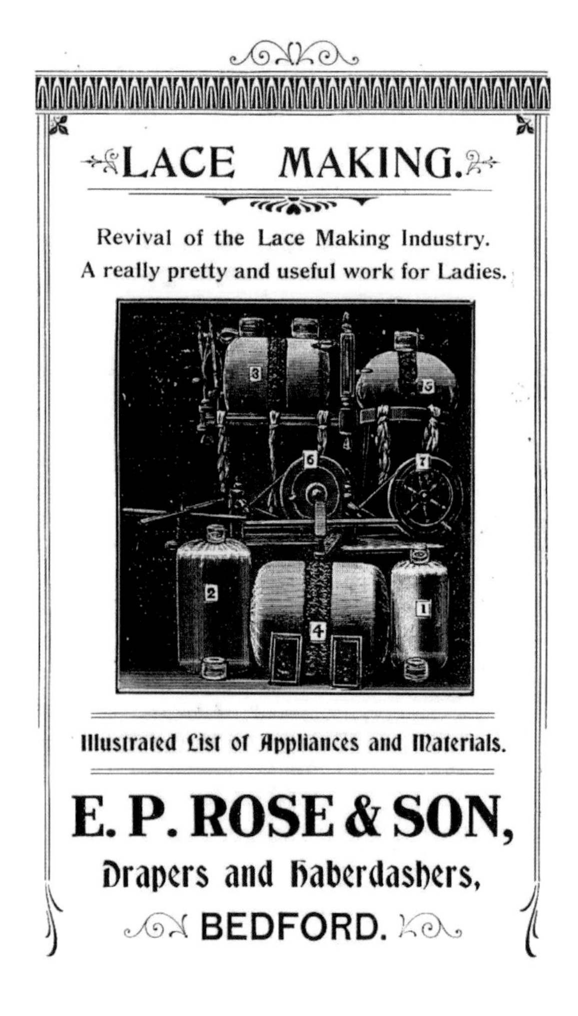
LACE MAKING.

Revival of the Lace Making Industry.
A really pretty and useful work for Ladies.

Illustrated List of Appliances and Materials.

E. P. ROSE & SON,
Drapers and Haberdashers,
BEDFORD.

Cover of 1910 Lace Catalogue

Prickings, thread, pins, Belgian and Ripon bobbins found in Mary Johnson's box [pillow is a modern miniature replica]

At some time, after the death of her husband Robert in 1911, Mary Johnson moved with her grandchildren to Coltsgate Hill. It is unclear when she began making lace, no evidence has been found that she did so prior to 1912, when the envelope containing the lace catalogue addresses her as, Mary Johnson, Pillow Lace Maker was sent. We cannot tell whether she learned the skill as a child, or had been inspired by the initiatives of recent exhibitions to revive the old crafts. The answers to these questions have been lost in time, but certainly many of the bobbins in her box were old enough to have been passed down through generations. We are grateful that her granddaughter Winifred kept this memento of her grandmother, and that they came back to Ripon.

Some samples of Mary Johnson's lace, pins and old Ripon bobbins [pillow is a modern miniature replica]

Following the First World War there is no information that the making of lace in Ripon continued in any way. It is not until the nineteen seventies that interest in the old craft began to grow once more.

Mary Johnson's lace samples showing the different designs available and their prices.

The prices range from sixpence (2½p) per yard to four shillings (20p) per yard

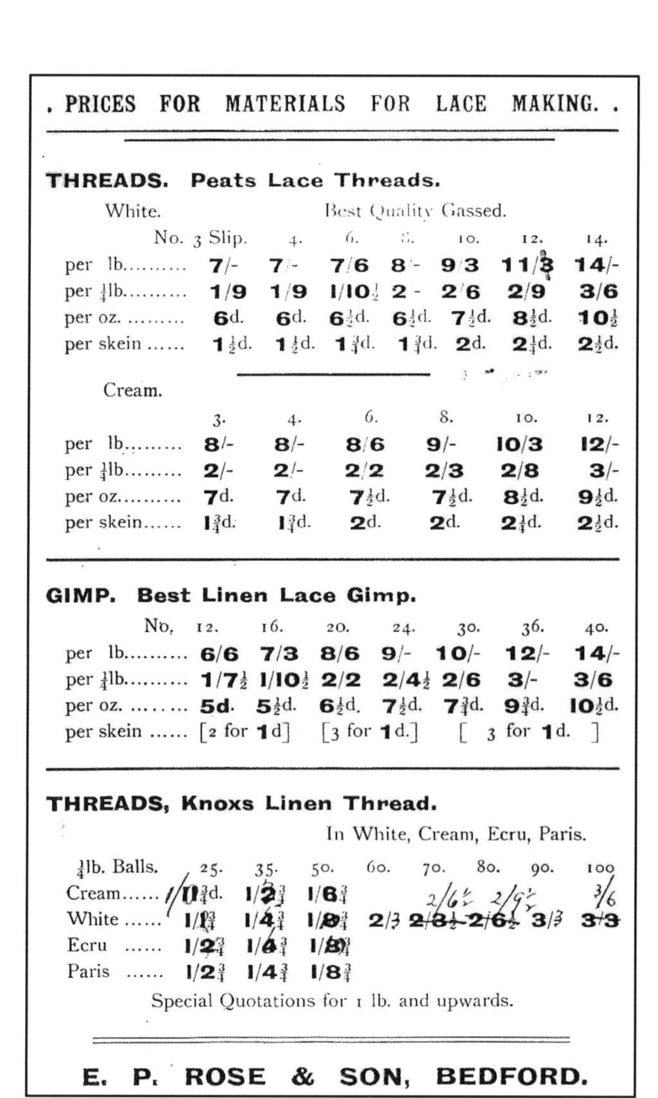

. PRICES FOR MATERIALS FOR LACE MAKING. .

THREADS. Peats Lace Threads.

White. Best Quality Gassed.

	No. 3 Slip.	4.	6.	8.	10.	12.	14.
per lb..........	7/-	7/-	7/6	8/-	9/3	11/3	14/-
per ¼lb..........	1/9	1/9	1/10½	2/-	2/6	2/9	3/6
per oz.	6d.	6d.	6½d.	6½d.	7½d.	8½d.	10½
per skein	1½d.	1½d.	1¾d.	1¾d.	2d.	2¼d.	2½d.

Cream.

	3.	4.	6.	8.	10.	12.
per lb.........	8/-	8/-	8/6	9/-	10/3	12/-
per ¼lb.........	2/-	2/-	2/2	2/3	2/8	3/-
per oz..........	7d.	7d.	7½d.	7½d.	8½d.	9½d.
per skein......	1¾d.	1¾d.	2d.	2d.	2¼d.	2½d.

GIMP. Best Linen Lace Gimp.

No.	12.	16.	20.	24.	30.	36.	40.
per lb..........	6/6	7/3	8/6	9/-	10/-	12/-	14/-
per ¼lb..........	1/7½	1/10½	2/2	2/4½	2/6	3/-	3/6
per oz.	5d.	5½d.	6½d.	7½d.	7¾d.	9¾d.	10½d.
per skein	[2 for 1d]		[3 for 1d.]		[3 for 1d.]		

THREADS, Knoxs Linen Thread.

In White, Cream, Ecru, Paris.

¼lb. Balls.	25.	35.	50.	60.	70.	80.	90.	100
Cream......	1/0¾d.	1/2¾	1/6¾		2/6½	2/9½		3/6
White	1/1¾	1/4¾	1/8¾	2/3	2/8½	2/6½	3/3	3/3
Ecru	1/2¾	1/4¾	1/8¾					
Paris	1/2¾	1/4¾	1/8¾					

Special Quotations for 1 lb. and upwards.

E. P. ROSE & SON, BEDFORD.

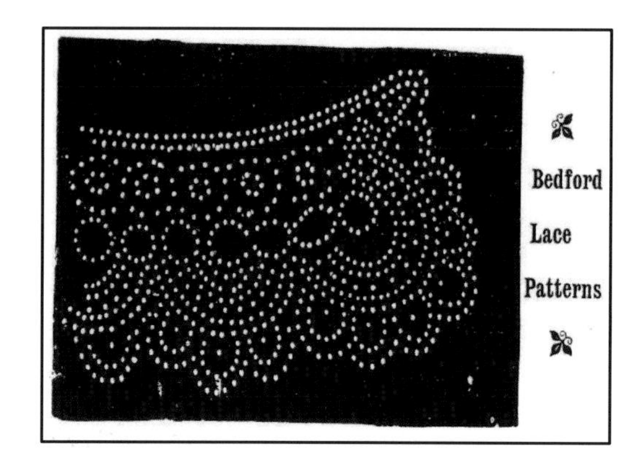

These illustrations show some of the items for sale, with their prices, as shown in the 1910 catalogue which belonged to Mary Johnson.

They show a selection of the wide range of materials offered by mail order in the early twentieth century.

E.P. ROSE & SON would seem to have been quite a prestigious firm who exhibited at the Ideal Home Exhibition at Olympia in London.

REQUISITES FOR LACE MAKING.

WOOD AND BONE BOBBINS.

	Doz.	Gross.
S12A	5½d. ...	5/-
S12B	5½d. ...	5/-
S12C	5½d. ...	5/-
S11	8½d. ..	7/6
S14	11d ...	10/6
S23	9½d. ...	9/-
S24	11d. ...	10/6
S13	8½d. ...	7/6
S10	10½d. ...	10/-
S21	11d. ...	10/6
S22	11d. ...	10/6
S15	1/8 ...	18/-
S17	1/8 ...	18/-
S18	1/10½ ...	21/-
S25	5/6 ...	60/-
S19	1/10½ ...	21/-
S20	1/10½ ...	21/-

Lace was also manufactured in other places in Yorkshire, and there are tantalising glimpses in the archives of some of those who were involved.

In York between 1774 and 1831, twenty six lace weavers were admitted as freemen of the city, allowing them to trade. Also in 1822 three lace manufacturers were trading.

The West Yorkshire Archive has two ornate indentures dated 1702 for girls apprenticed to bone lace maker Mary Thornton of Wakefield. Records also show in 1703 a soldier's wife from Halifax applied for a certificate to travel about the country to sell her bone lace to help maintain herself and her three children, and in 1709, also at Wakefield, a licensed traveller in bone lace applied for an affidavit so he would be protected from recruitment. At Wakefield Quarter Sessions in 1718, a lace seller who was robbed was reimbursed by the court following evidence given by witnesses.

Hull City Archives records William Locking, a lace manufacturer of Hull, agreeing to the terms of a lease on the fifth of May 1834. The property is described as a messuage on the south side of Silver Street, formerly the Mermaid Public House. The term of the lease was for fourteen years, and the rent forty two pounds per annum.

There does not appear to be any evidence that would show that these other areas had any sort of lace industry which was as substantial, or which covered as long a period of time as that in Ripon.

In more recent times there has been a revival of many of the old crafts that were lost with the coming of the Industrial Revolution. In the nineteen seventies Mrs Scott began classes at Grantley Hall for the West Riding Education Authority, to teach the making of bobbin lace, and in 1978 Miss V. Broadley began teaching bobbin lacemaking at Ripon Adult Education classes. These were now purely for recreational purposes.

1986 Hobbies Exhibition in Hugh Ripley Hall with Wendy Cole, Beechy Jarrett and Veronica Broadley

When writing an article for The Dalesman in 1983, Carson I.A. Ritchie received a letter from Mrs May Gill of Harrogate. The information she gave was of great interest and told of a time, sixty years earlier, when she had been at school in Ripon and had met a very old lady who lived on Bondgate who was said to be "the last of the lacemakers in Ripon". She also remembered exhibits in The Wakeman's House of lacemaking artifacts, including samples of lace of various patterns, and bobbins which were similar to Honiton bobbins, but smaller and thicker. These were made of fruitwoods and unspangled. Mrs Gill herself had a very old Ripon lace pillow, with pins made from wire and sealing wax. She also spoke of pins that were made of fish bones, and some of goosegrass thorns. The letter concluded by saying that Beeston, near Leeds, had once been another centre for making lace.

In November of 1985, North Yorkshire Local History Advisor Mrs June Hall arranged that groups of children from schools in the Ripon area would meet, on alternate Wednesday afternoons, and begin to learn to make lace for a heritage exhibition the following year. There was a great deal of enthusiasm for the scheme, with teachers and parents becoming involved. The children learned quickly and soon gained the required skills.

The Festival in 1986 was to celebrate the one hundred year anniversary of the Millenary Festival that had been held in Ripon in 1886. Various events and exhibitions were held during the year. In March of 1986 an exhibition showing hobbies was held in Hugh Ripley Hall, where many unusual and creative crafts were demonstrated. Some of the ladies who had been instrumental in the revival of the making of bobbin lace in Ripon gave demonstrations of lacemaking, and showed some of their work.

On the 16th May 1986 the Environmental Heritage Exhibition was opened in the Cathedral by Lord Asa Briggs. It was here that the impressive collection of lace made by the schoolchildren was displayed. The children demonstrated their skills, working at their lace pillows, and wearing costumes from the eighteenth and nineteenth centuries.

It was hoped that the enthusiasm that had been created, and the skills learned, would encourage the making of lace to continue in Ripon into the twenty-first century.

21st CENTURY

So we come to the present day. We have taken a look at the past to find the place where Ripon stood in the history of lacemaking. The information has at best been sketchy, and without our unexpected gift of lacemaking artefacts we would not have achieved this book. We have filled the gaps between the facts with our theories. We hope that these will encourage the reader to speculate further, inspire the search for more evidence, and perhaps one day discover even more of the truth.

Still today in Ripon and the surrounding area there are groups of lacemakers, who come together in friendship to enjoy the craft of making lace. They do this to share their knowledge and for the pleasure it gives them to create something of great beauty, and they are highly skilled.

Evelyn Burnell   Mary Ellis   Christine Wood   Jill Clark   Wendy Cole

To one such group we are highly indebted. The ladies in the photograph above are those who gave their time and expertise to unravel the mysteries of the old parchment prickings, and produce the patterns from the past we have published so far, without their help it would not have been possible.

For the future, we cannot know, but with the enthusiasm to be found in those involved in today's groups of lacemakers, there is no doubt that this ancient craft has every chance to continue and form the next strand in the history of lacemaking in Ripon.

THE PATTERNS

Winding trails that bind the years

And precious pearls of happiness;

Twists that brought their pain and tears,

All these her silent thoughts caress.

Sitting placidly by the door

A soothing sound the bobbins make,

But memory's barque must come ashore

'Tis evening and the shadows break

A R Elliott

The patterns numbered OR were found in research material belonging to the late Beechy F. Jarratt. Most of them were originally reproduced for an Exhibition held in Ripon in 1986 where they were presented as being old Ripon Lace patterns although we have been unable to find any tangible evidence to support this suggestion.

It can be seen that the popular honeycomb ground is predominant but all of the patterns echo other styles of lace such as Bucks Point, Lille and Torchon. MJ5, MJ6, MJ7 and MJ12 are known to have been worked in Ripon and MJ3 was known locally as the Four Penny Spot.

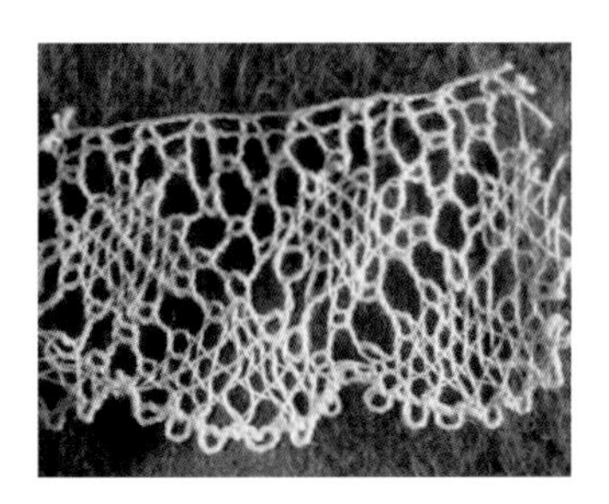

Four Penny Spot worked by Mary Johnson

Patterns numbered MJ have been re-drafted either from samples of lace or prickings that were found in Mary Johnson's box. Some of them were marked with a selling price per yard and although it is unclear as to which year(s) this price referred it must have been before Mary Johnson's death in 1914. Most of the patterns are easily recognised as Torchon or Bedfordshire and will doubtless have been made in many parts of the British Isles under local names with each lacemaker using their own techniques and choice of stitches. A few of the prickings closely relate to the finer Bucks Point, Lille and Tønder styles of lace which are worked with a net ground and a more active gimp. However, the fact that these patterns were being produced in Ripon around the turn of the 1900's suggests that the type of lace being made there was being influenced by the style and trends at that time.

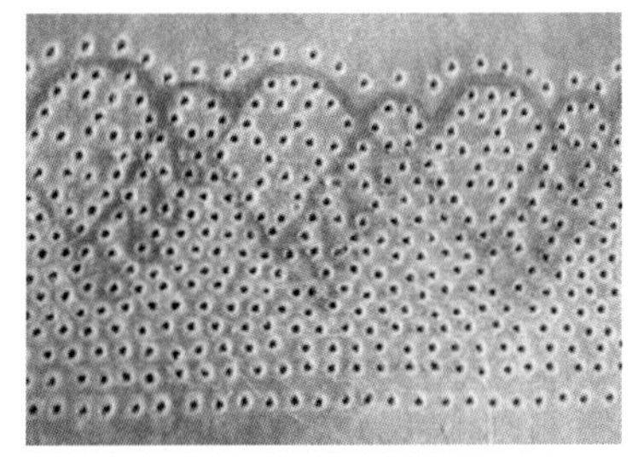

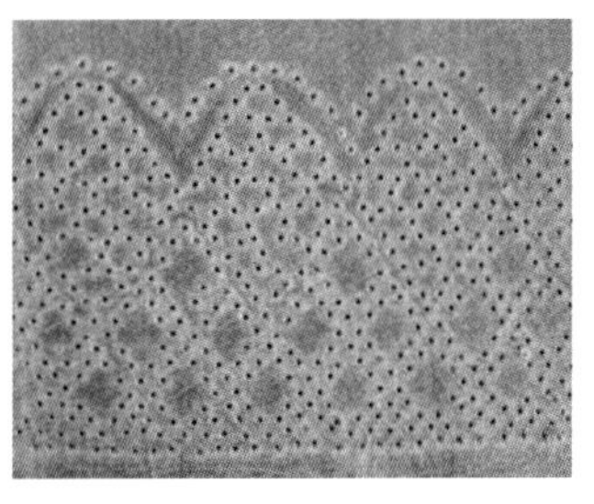

Examples of finer prickings found in the "Box"

The lace shown with each of the patterns numbered MJ has mainly been worked according to the techniques applied by Mary Johnson. Her extensive use of half stitch suggests that it was a great favourite and she had her own unique method of working spiders which actually had more legs than the pricking catered for. This method has not been repeated in any other lace that we are aware of and as the "floating legs" do not exactly enhance the overall effect the traditional method of working spiders has been used to work the patterns throughout this book. Where no lace sample was evident, only a pricking, we have referred to comparable examples found in museum collections or, in some cases, an assortment of working methods for a particular design has been proposed.

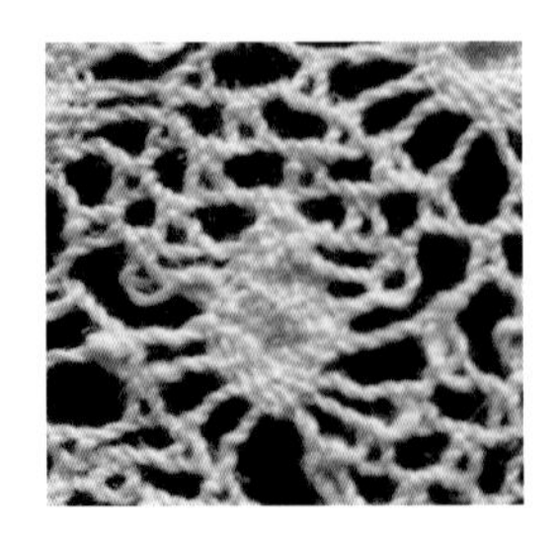

Mary Johnson's unique spider

There are two patterns numbered HM which have been redrafted and worked according to examples held in the Harrogate Museums and Arts lace collection. Although neither was identified as being of any specific style of lace HM1 is of great interest because of its pronounced resemblance to Scotland's Hamilton Lace and also to some very detailed instructions given on pages 2388-2390 in an (unknown) encyclopaedia under a section headed "Lace".

The encyclopaedia shows drawings of un-spangled lace bobbins, which appear to be identical to the traditional fruit wood bobbins used in Ripon, and states that "*Ripon Lace is another simple pattern which the amateur may learn with advantage, for it provides one with an expert knowledge of the fundamental stitches of pillow lace.*" The instructions given in this encyclopaedia were followed exactly by Jean Leader who used it to produce the handkerchief and the concise technical drawing shown below, details of which were published by the Lace Guild in "Lace No 83" (1996).

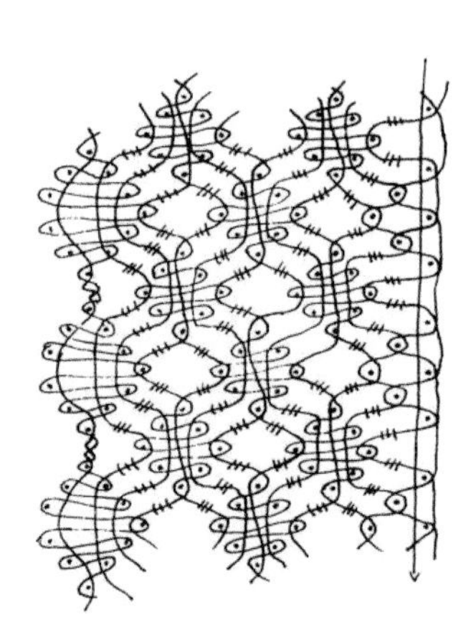

Ripon Lace *Photo: Jean Leader*

The same diamond shape blocks separated by 3 twist bars were used to work the Hamilton Lace although the edge of this lace appears to use another pattern rather than a fan. The piece of lace, opposite, held in the Harrogate Museums and Arts lace collection is not dissimilar in design to the beautiful Hamilton Lace collar that can be found on display in Hamilton Museum.

Courtesy of Harrogate Museums & Arts

Photo: Jean Leader

Hamilton Lace collar
Courtesy of South Lanarkshire Council Museum Department

Finally you will find a pricking together with a technical drawing for the "Ripon Horn" which is pictured on the book cover. Inspired by Harker's Original Crochet Pattern No 8 it was designed to be worked in Binche Lace by Mary Moseley with much help and encouragement from Anne-Marie Verbeke Billiet.

With the exception of the Ripon Horn, the prickings and technical drawings have been reproduced with the aid of ILSOFT Ltd lace R-XP.

OR1

A quick and simple narrow edge.

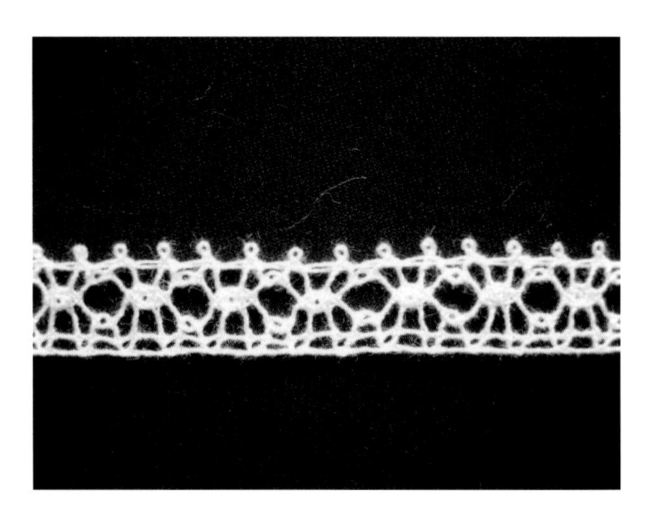

Thread:	36/2 Brok Cotton
Bobbins:	7 pairs
Headside:	1 passive pair worked in cloth stitch + picot.
Spiders:	Twist legs 3 times.
Ground:	Double stitch, pin, double stitch.
Footside:	1 passive pair worked in double stitch and an extra twist on the worker. The edge stitch is worked in double stitch with an extra twist on the worker and 2 extra twists on outside edge pair. Work double stitch back through the passive pair plus :- 1 extra twist on the passive and 2 extra twists on the worker if passing into the spider or 1 extra twist on the passive pair only if passing into ground.

Double stitch *= Cloth stitch +1 twist on both pairs*

OR1

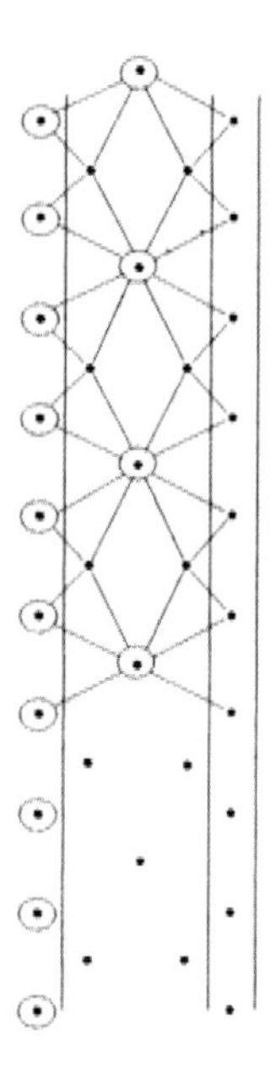

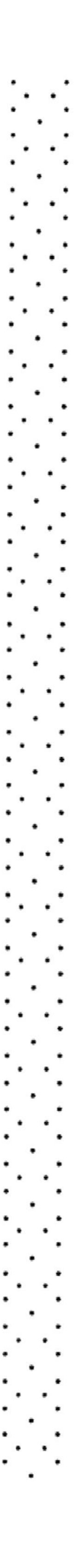

OR2

The gimp that outlines the honeycomb heart continues to work the tree fan by weaving through the passives.

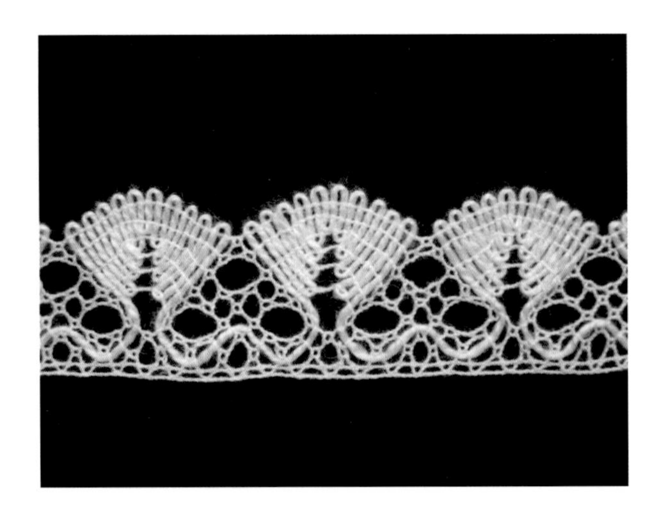

Thread:	60/2 Brok Cotton DMC Cotton Perle No 5
Bobbins:	11 pairs
Gimp:	1 bobbin
Fan:	2 twists between weaving gimp and 3 twists between the centre veins.
Hearts:	Honeycomb.
Ground:	Half stitch + 1 twist, pin, half stitch + 2 twists.
Footside:	1 passive pair worked in double stitch with an extra twist on the worker. The edge stitch is worked in double stitch with an extra twist on the worker and 2 extra twists on outside edge pair. Work double stitch back through the passive pair + 2 extra twists on the worker and + 1 extra twist on the passive.

Double stitch = Cloth stitch +1 twist on both pairs

OR2

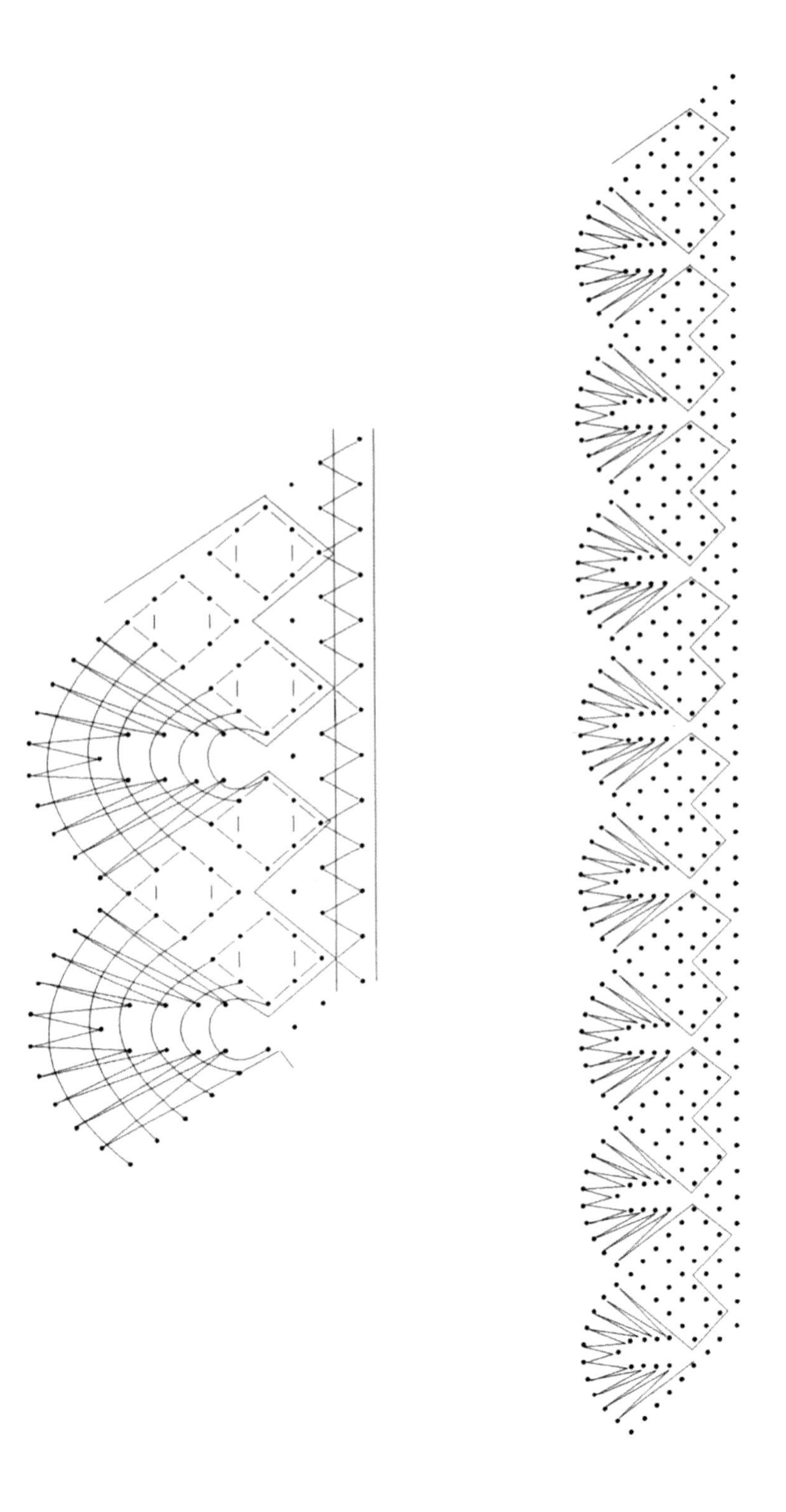

OR3

This pricking can be used to produce two very different patterns. Both are worked with the same headside, only the inner design varies.
Pattern A – Worked with 3 cloth stitch diamonds
Pattern B – A gimp outlines the honeycomb rings.

Pattern A

Thread:	70/2 Egyptian Cotton
Bobbins:	11 pairs
Headside:	2 passive pairs worked in cloth stitch + a picot.
Diamonds:	Cloth stitch with 2 or 3 twists depending on length of bars.
Footside:	1 passive pair worked in double stitch with an extra twist on the worker. The edge stitch is worked in double stitch with an extra twist on the worker and 2 extra twists on outside edge pair. Work double stitch back through the passive pair + 1 extra twist on both pairs.

Pattern B

Thread:	70/2 Egyptian Cotton DMC Cotton Perle No 8
Bobbins:	12 pairs
Gimp:	1 pair
Headside:	2 passive pairs worked in cloth stitch + a picot.
Hearts:	Honeycomb.
Footside:	2 passive pairs worked in cloth stitch + 2 twists on the worker. The edge stitch is worked in double stitch with an extra twist on the worker and 2 extra twists on outside edge pair. Work cloth stitch back through the passive pairs + 2 twists on the worker before passing through the gimp.

Double stitch *= Cloth stitch +1 twist on both pairs*

OR3

Pattern A

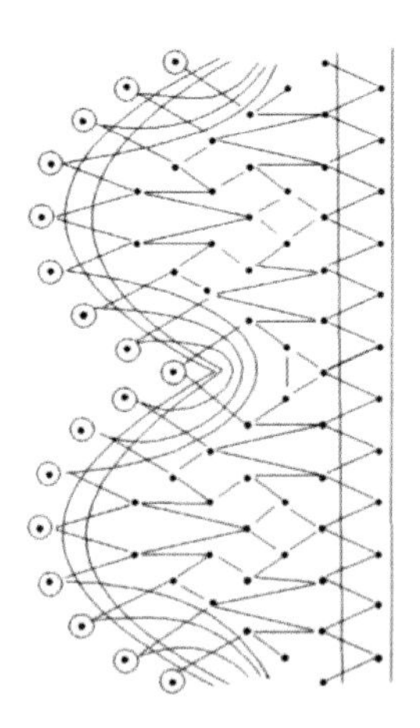

Pattern B

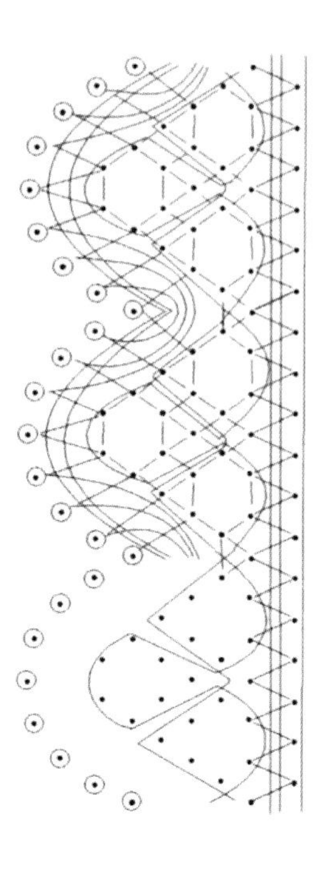

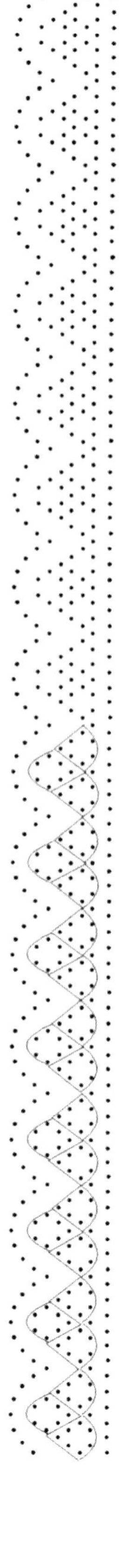

OR4

A pretty edging with an inverted fan and honeycomb ground.

Thread:	60/2 Brok Cotton
Bobbins:	11 pairs
Headside:	Cloth stitch with a double stitch edge + an extra twist round the pin.
Ground:	Honeycomb.
Footside:	1 passive pair worked in double stitch and an extra twist on the worker. The edge stitch is worked in double stitch with an extra twist on the worker and 2 extra twists on the outside edge pair. Work double stitch back through the passive pair + 1 extra twist on both pairs.

Double stitch = *Cloth stitch +1 twist on both pairs*

OR4

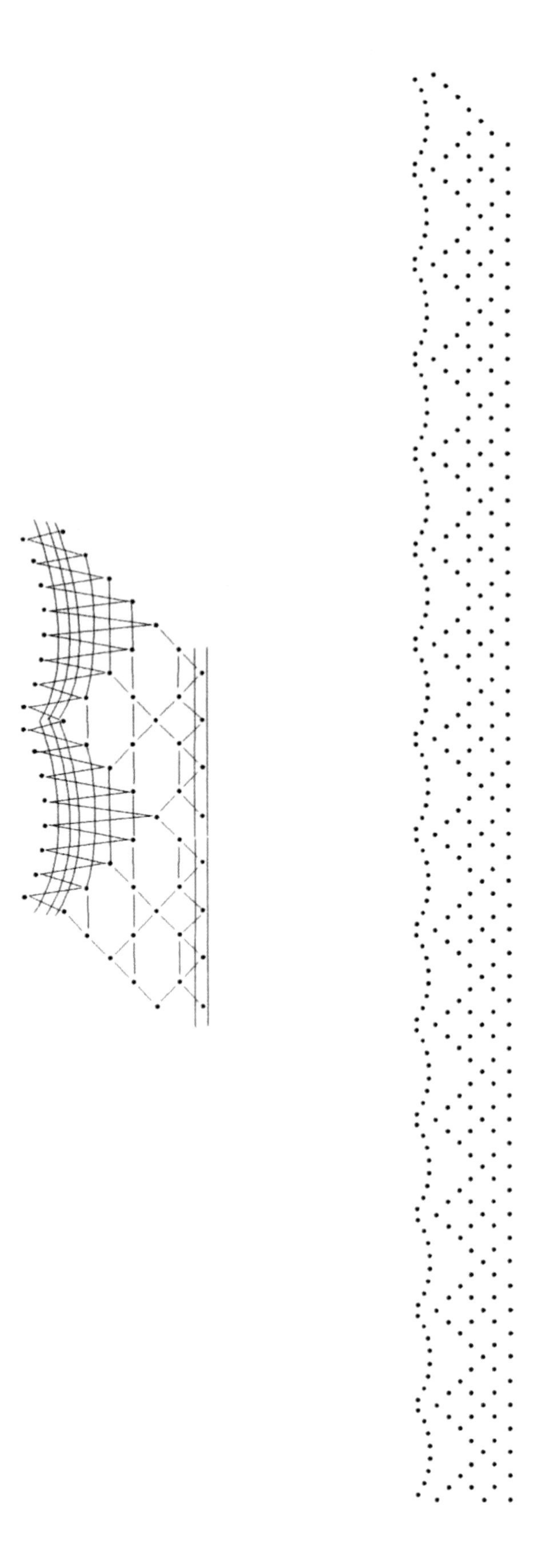

OR5

An unusual net ground pattern that relies on the gimps to define the sparse shapes. The subject of the design is open to personal interpretation.

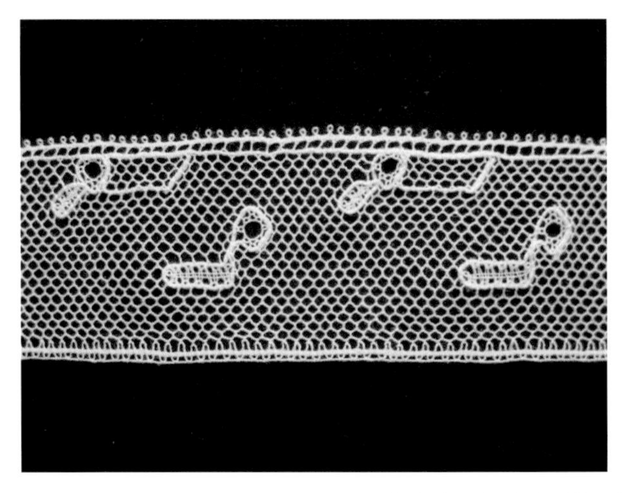

Worked by Christine Wood

Thread:	120/2 Egyptian Cotton DMC Cotton Perle No 12
Bobbins:	29 pairs
Gimps:	2 pairs + 1 bobbin
Headside:	2 passive pairs worked in cloth stitch + a picot with twists on either side of the gimp.
Duck shape:	Cloth stitch and honeycomb.
Turtle shape:	Cloth stitch, honeycomb and net ground.
Ground:	Net ground.
Footside:	2 pairs of passives worked in cloth stitch with a catch stitch on the inside edge.

Net ground = *half stitch + 2 twists pinned between the twisted pairs.*

Catch stitch = *pin is placed to the right of the twisted pairs instead of between them.*

OR5

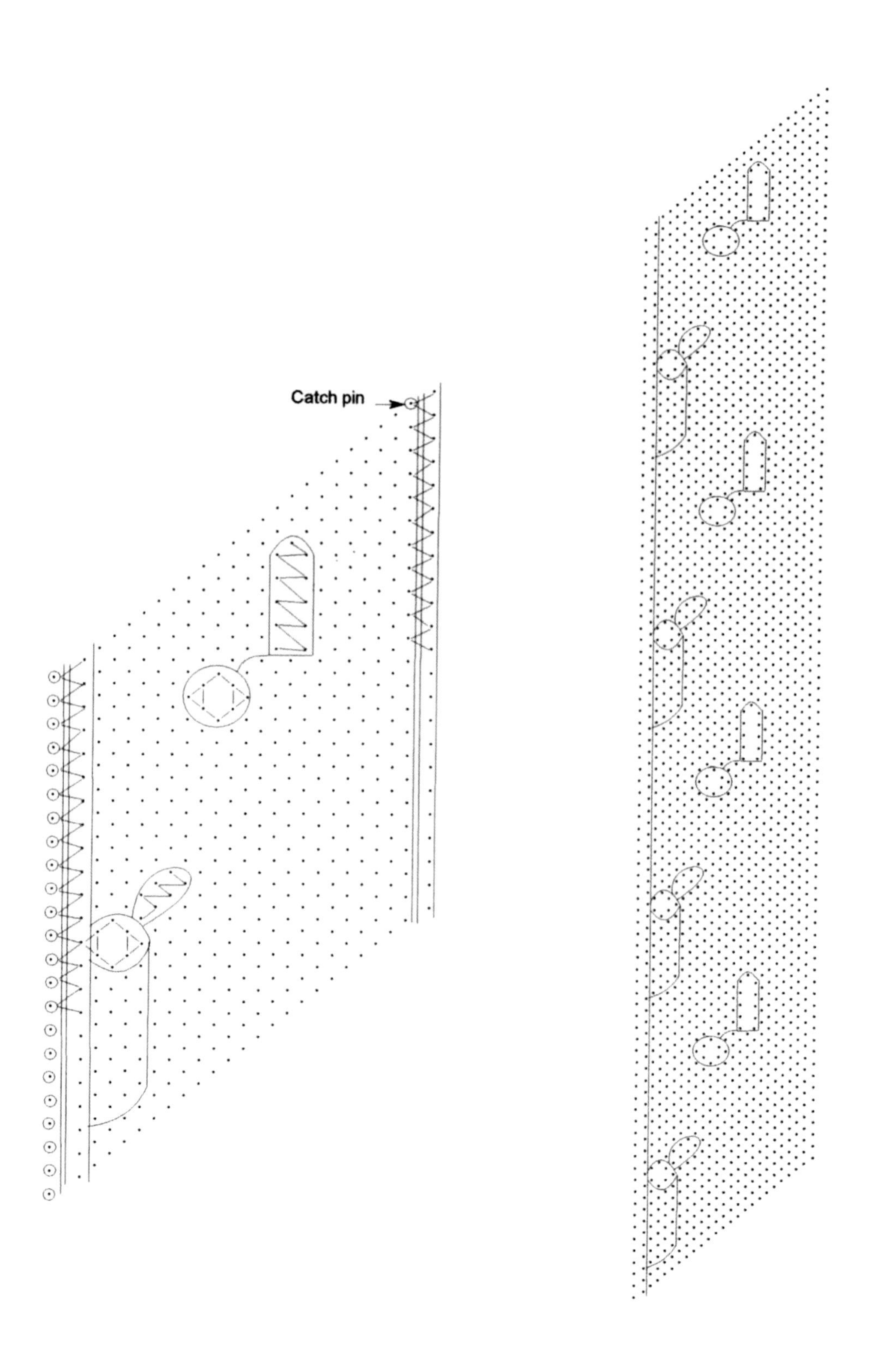

MJ1

Mary Johnson had worked her sample in linen thread but the pattern works equally well in 36/2 Brok Cotton.

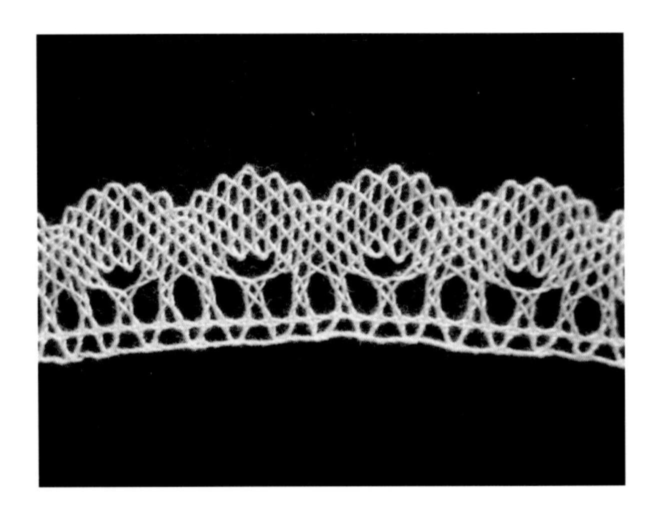

Thread:	36/2 Brok Cotton
Bobbins:	8 pairs
Fan:	Half stitch.
Ground:	Half stitch, pin, half stitch.
Footside:	1 passive pair worked in double stitch and an extra twist on the worker. The edge stitch is worked in double stitch with an extra twist on the worker and 2 extra twists on outside edge pair. Work double stitch back through the passive pair.

MJ1

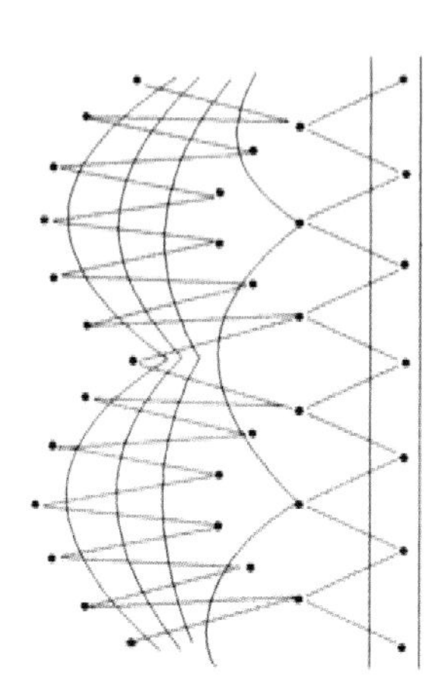

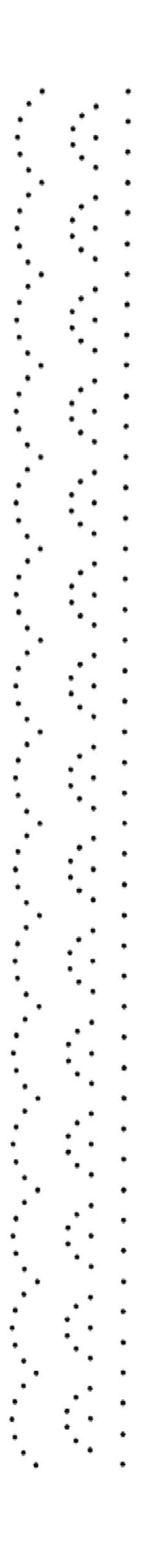

MJ2

Only a pricking was found for this charming narrow heart insertion which can be worked using different stitches with or without a gimp.

Thread:	60/2 Brok Cotton DMC Cotton Perle No 5 (optional)
Bobbins:	13 pairs
Gimps:	1 pair (optional)
Hearts:	Cloth stitch or half stitch.
Ground:	Half stitch + 1 twist, pin, half stitch + 2 twists.
Footside:	1 passive pair worked in double stitch and an extra twist on the worker. The edge stitch is worked in double stitch with an extra twist on the worker and 2 extra twists on outside edge pair. Work double stitch back through the passive pair + 2 twists on the worker and + 1 twist on the passive.

Double stitch *= Cloth stitch +1 twist on both pairs*

MJ2

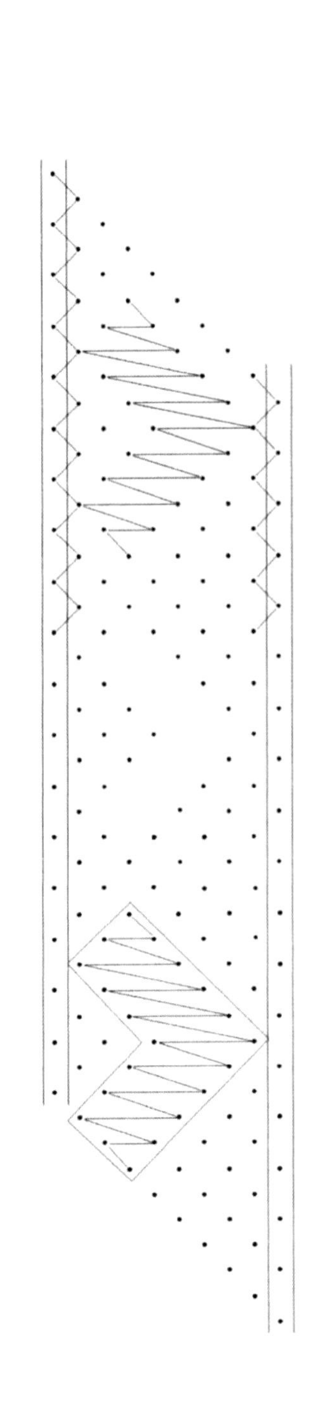

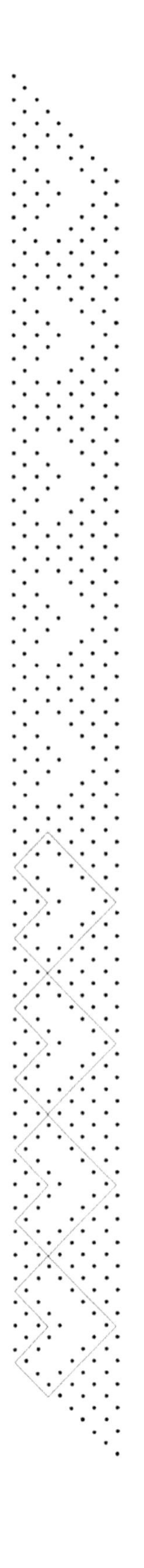

MJ3

Locally known as the "Four Penny Spot" it was reputedly one of the last known patterns to be made in the City. Mary Johnson's sample was priced at 9 pence a yard and corresponds to No 455, of the same name, in the Palliser Collection housed at Exeter's Royal Albert Museum.

Thread:	60/2 Brok Cotton
Bobbins:	13 pairs
Fan:	Half stitch with a double stitch edge and an extra twist round the pin.
Diamonds:	Half stitch.
Ground:	Half stitch + 1 twist, pin, half stitch + 2 twists.
Footside:	1 passive pair worked in double stitch and an extra twist on the worker. The edge stitch is worked in double stitch with an extra twist on the worker and 2 extra twists on outside edge pair. Work double stitch back through the passive pair + 2 twists on the worker and + 1 twist on the passive.

Double stitch *= Cloth stitch +1 twist on both pairs*

MJ3

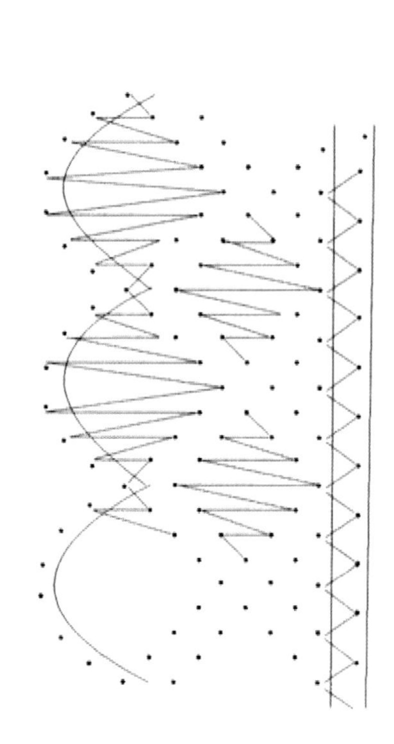

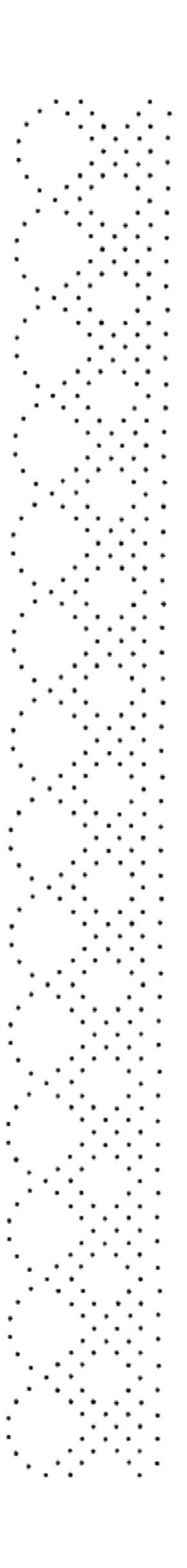

MJ4

A wide edging that is very similar to an insertion found in the Kent Collection housed at Harrogate Museums & Arts. Mary Johnson's small sample was worked in a linen thread and she had unexpectedly edged her tree fan with a plait.

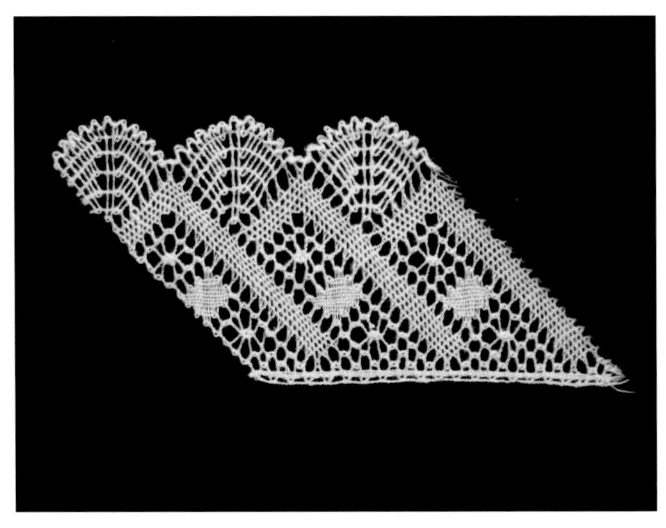

Worked by Jill Clark

Thread:	60/2 Brockens Linen
Bobbins:	27 pairs
Fan:	Double stitch tree fan with a plait running round the outer edge changing pairs at the top of the fan.
Trail:	Half stitch.
Diamonds:	Cloth stitch.
Spiders:	Twist legs 4 times
Ground:	Double stitch, pin, double stitch.
Footside:	2 passive pairs worked in cloth stitch with 1 twist on the worker. The edge stitch is worked in double stitch with 2 extra twists on outside edge pair. Work cloth stitch back through the passive pairs and twist the worker once.

Double stitch *= Cloth stitch +1 twist on both pairs*

MJ4

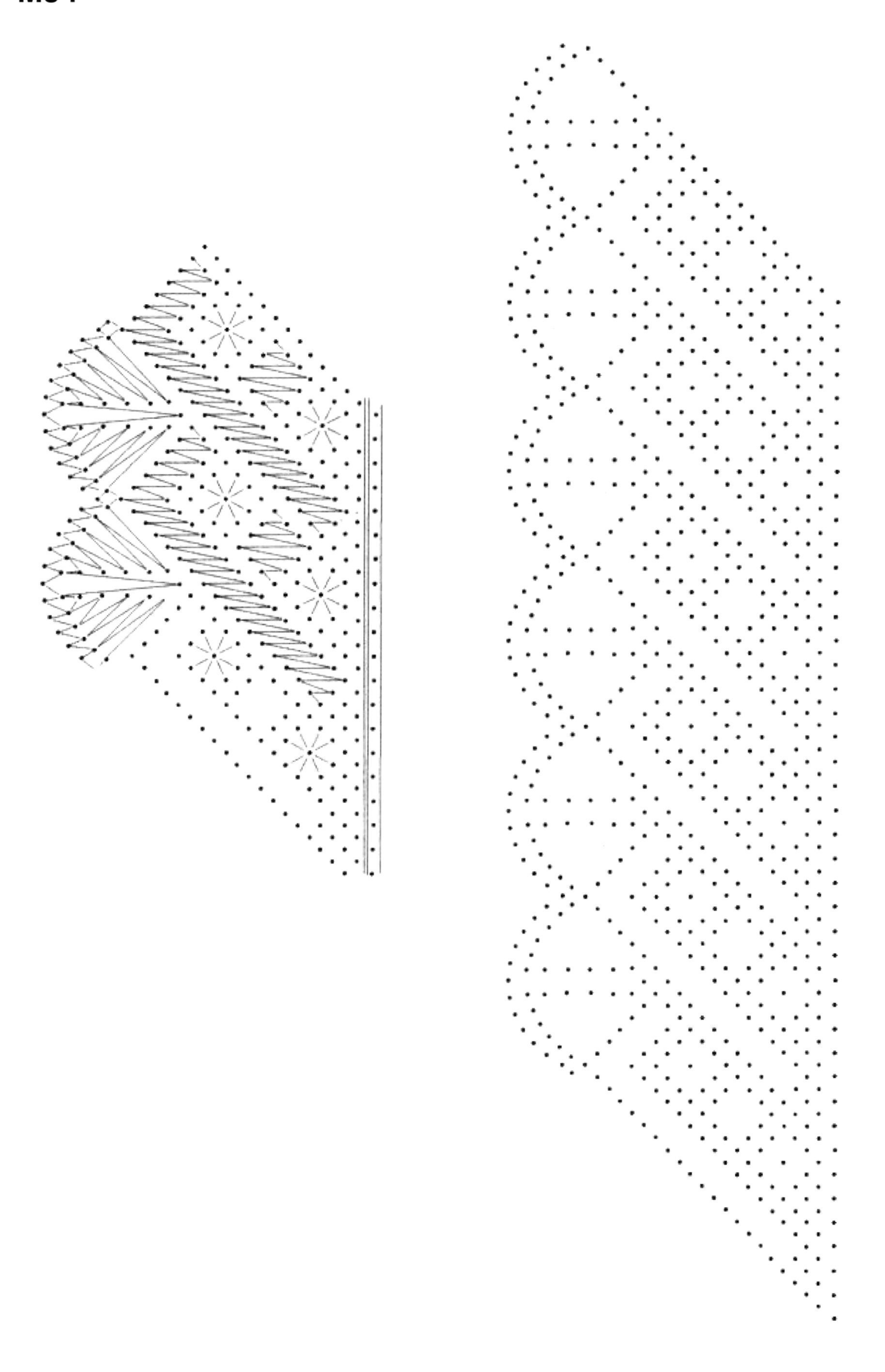

MJ5

A simple insertion very much like edging No 458 in the Palliser Collection housed at the Royal Albert Museum in Exeter and also an edging in the Kent Collection at Harrogate Museums and Arts. Mary Johnson's original lace sample was priced at 8 shillings a yard.

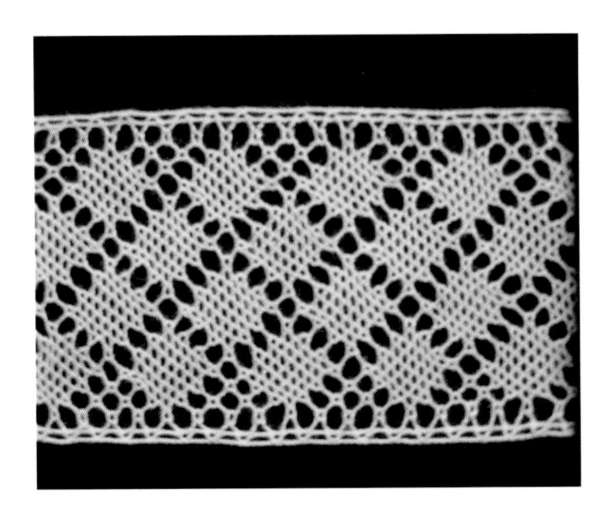

Thread:	60/2 Brok Cotton
Bobbins:	24 pairs
Diamonds:	Half stitch with 3 twists between them.
Ground:	Half stitch + 1 twist, pin, half stitch + 2 twists.
Footside:	1 passive pair worked in double stitch with an extra twist on the worker. The edge stitch is worked in double stitch with an extra twist on the worker and 2 extra twists on outside edge pair. Work double stitch back through the passive pair + 2 twists on the worker and + 1 twist on the passive.

Double stitch *= Cloth stitch +1 twist on both pairs*

MJ5

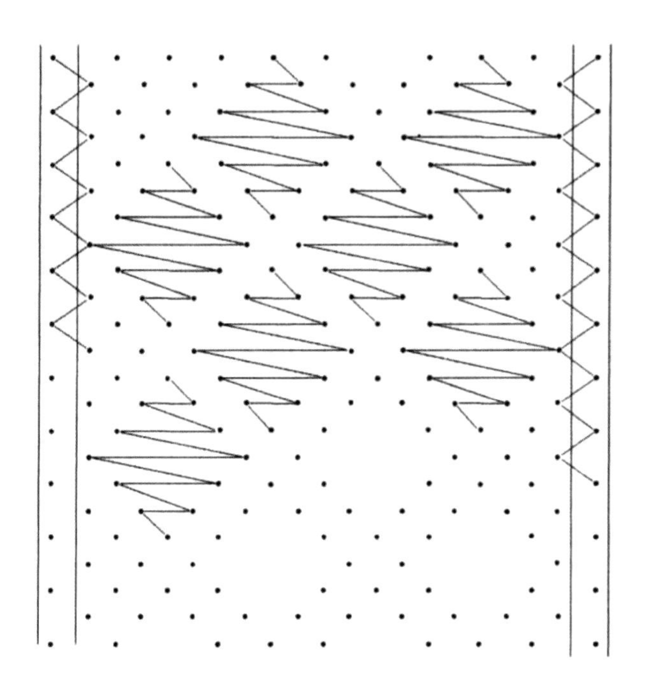

MJ6

The sample, which was priced at 8 shillings & 9 pence a yard, is similar to No 457 in the Palliser Collection housed at Exeter's Royal Albert Museum and also to the lace in the photograph that accompanied Carson I A Ritchie's article on Yorkshire Lace which was published in The Dalesman (1983). In both instances the choice of stitches differs from those used by Mary Johnson.

Thread:	60/2 Brok Cotton
Bobbins:	26 pairs
Fan:	Half stitch with a double stitch edge and an extra twist round the pin.
Diamonds:	Half stitch.
Spiders:	Twist legs 4 times.
Ground:	Half stitch + 1 twist, pin, half stitch + 2 twists.
Footside:	1 passive pair worked in double stitch and an extra twist on the worker. The edge stitch is worked in double stitch with an extra twist on the worker and 2 extra twists on outside edge pair. Work double stitch back through the passive pair + 2 twists on the worker and + 1 twist on the passive.

***Double stitch** = Cloth stitch +1 twist on both pairs*

MJ6

MJ7

Mary Johnson's lace sample was priced 2 shillings & 6 pence a yard. This pattern, albeit worked with different stitches, equates to No 452 in the Palliser Collection housed at the Royal Albert Museum in Exeter.

Thread:	60/2 Brok Cotton
Bobbins:	20 pairs
Fan:	Half stitch with a double stitch edge and an extra twist round the pin.
Diamonds:	Half stitch.
Spiders:	Twist legs 4 times.
Ground:	Half stitch + 1 twist, pin, half stitch + 2 twists.
Footside:	1 passive pair worked in double stitch and an extra twist on the worker. The edge stitch is worked in double stitch with an extra twist on the worker and 2 extra twists on outside edge pair. Work double stitch back through the passive pair + 2 twists on the worker and + 1 twist on the passive.

Double stitch *= Cloth stitch +1 twist on both pairs*

MJ7

MJ8

The original lace sample, priced by Mary Johnson at 3 shillings a yard, was worked in a slightly finer thread to some of the other designs.

Thread:	70/2 Egyptian Cotton
Bobbins:	27 pairs
Fan:	Cloth stitch with a double stitch edge and an extra twist round the pin.
Trail:	Cloth stitch.
Diamonds:	Half stitch.
Ground:	Half stitch + 1 twist, pin, half stitch + 2 twists.
Footside:	1 passive pair worked in double stitch and an extra twist on the worker. The edge stitch is worked in double stitch with an extra twist on the worker and 2 extra twists on outside edge pair. Work double stitch back through the passive pair + 2 twists on the worker and + 1 twist on the passive.

Double stitch *= Cloth stitch +1 twist on both pairs*

MJ8

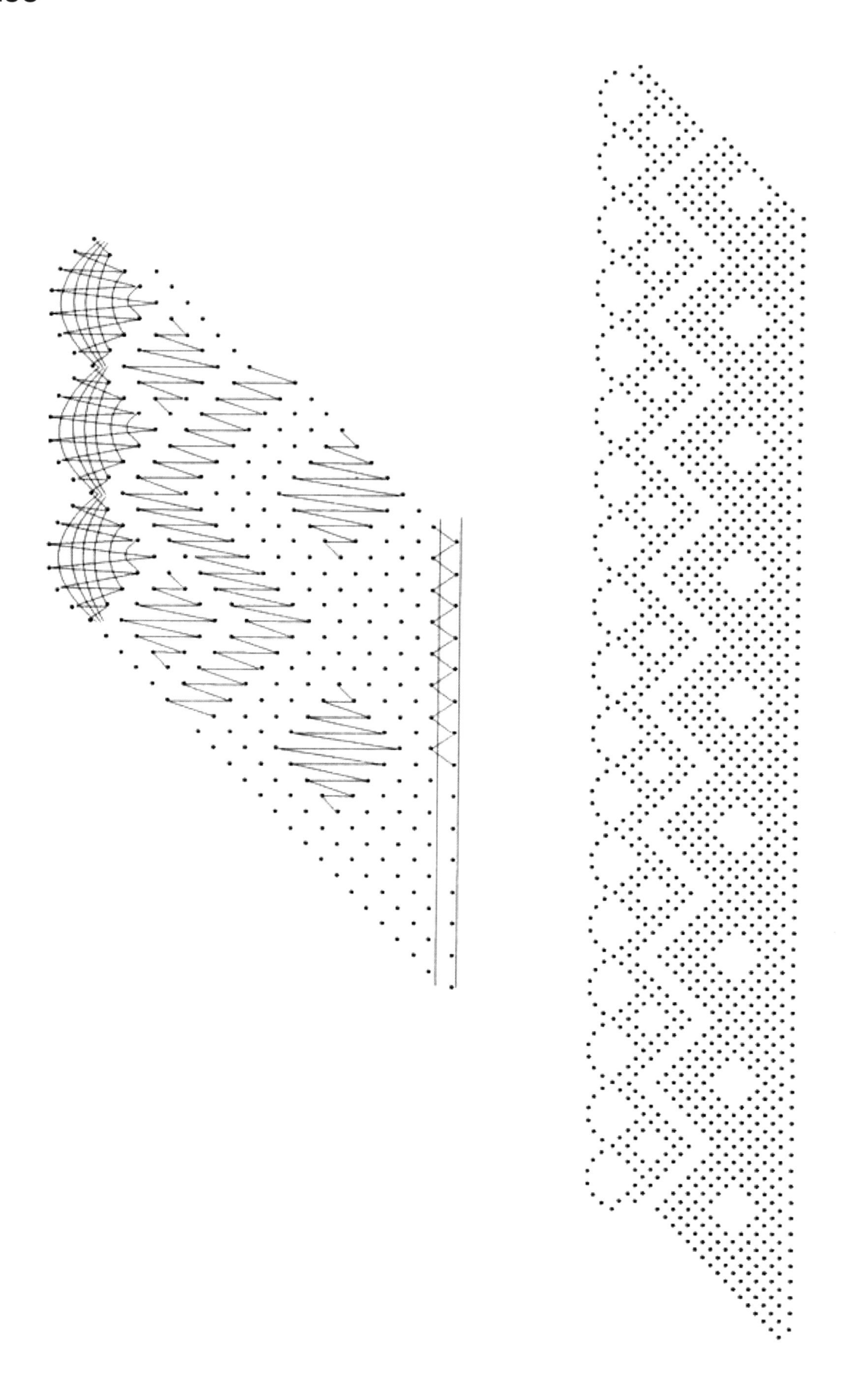

MJ9

A somewhat distorted pricking and lace sample priced at 2 shillings & 9 pence a yard was found for this unusual design. The lace has an exceptionally deep fan and an alternative footside technique.

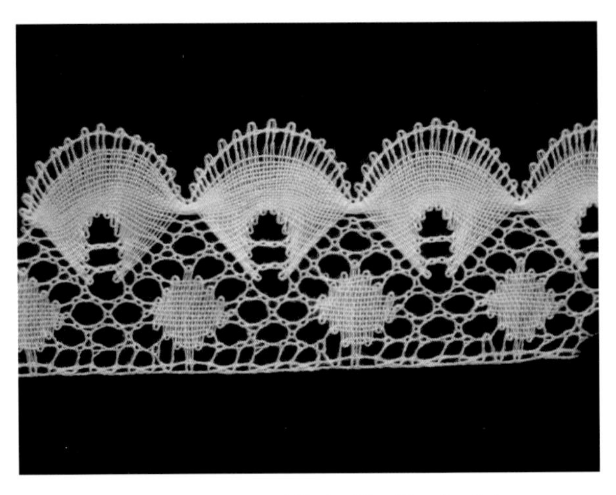

Worked by Wendy Cole

Thread:	50 Tanne.
Bobbins:	23 pairs.
Fan:	Cloth stitch with a double stitch edge and an extra twist round the pin.
Diamonds:	Cloth stitch.
Ground:	Honeycomb.
Footside:	From the Honeycomb:- 1 passive pair worked in double stitch and an extra twist on the worker. The edge stitch is worked in double stitch with an extra twist round the pin and 2 extra twists on outside edge pair. Work double stitch back through the passive pair + 1 extra twist on both pairs. From the Diamond: - 1 passive pair worked in cloth stitch with 2 twists on the worker. The edge stitch is worked in double stitch with an extra twist on the worker and 2 extra twists on outside edge pair. Work cloth stitch back through the passive pair and twist the passive pair twice.

Mary Johnson's sample was worked using the footside shown in the photograph and on the technical drawing at A but the pattern works equally as well using the more traditional method.

Double stitch *= Cloth stitch +1 twist on both pairs*

MJ9

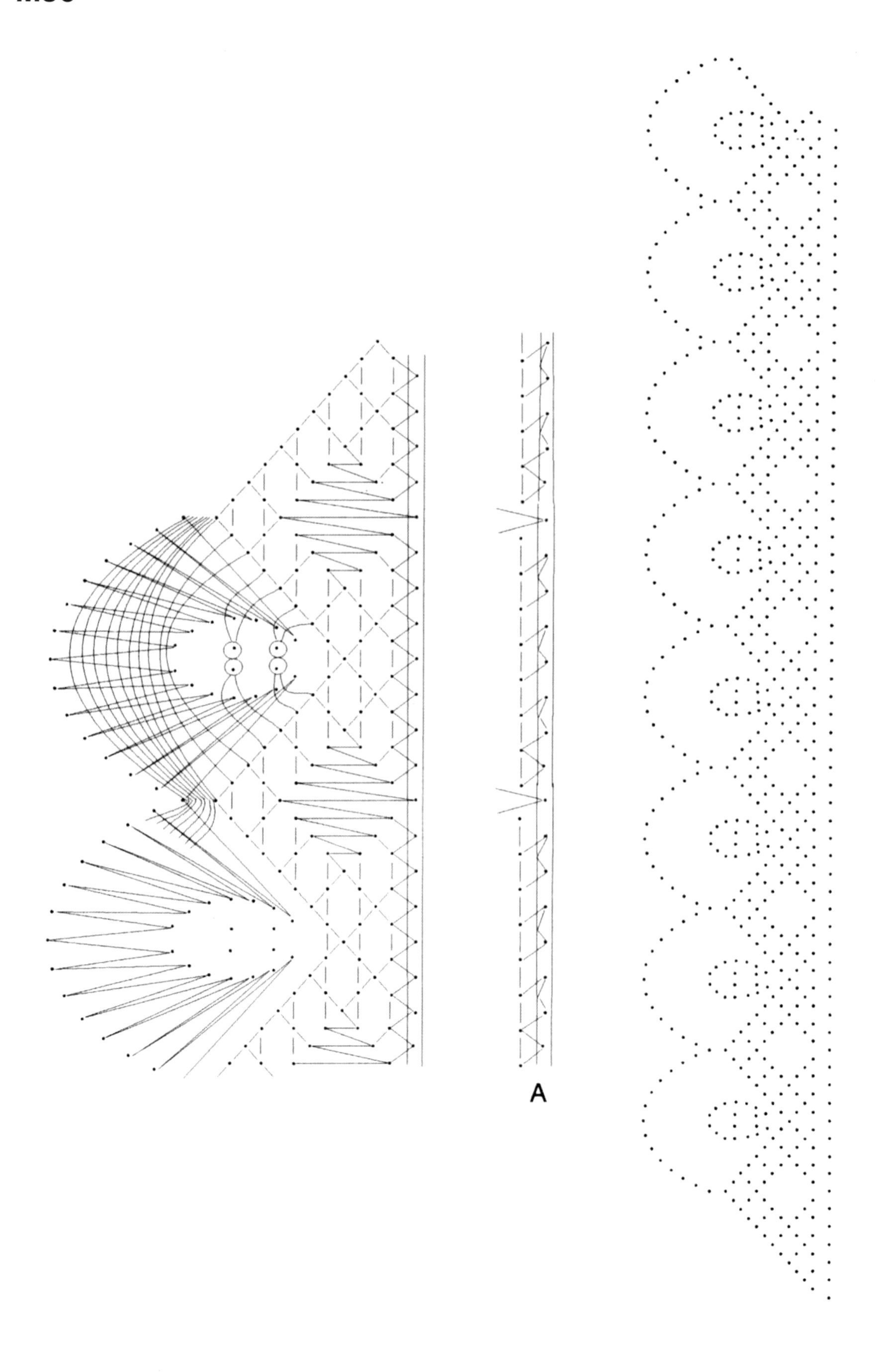

MJ10

This attractive insertion is worked with a net ground and gimps that outline the intricate shapes. It echoes No 15 'Garland' one of the original laces based on old Flemish patterns worked in the Tønder style found in Johnanne Nyrop-Larsen's book 'Knipling efter Tegning' (1955). A similar pattern albeit without the honeycomb diamond can also be seen in a piece of lace in the Kent Collection at Harrogate Museums and Arts.

As no example of worked lace was available the sample shown here suggests different fillings for some of the shapes.

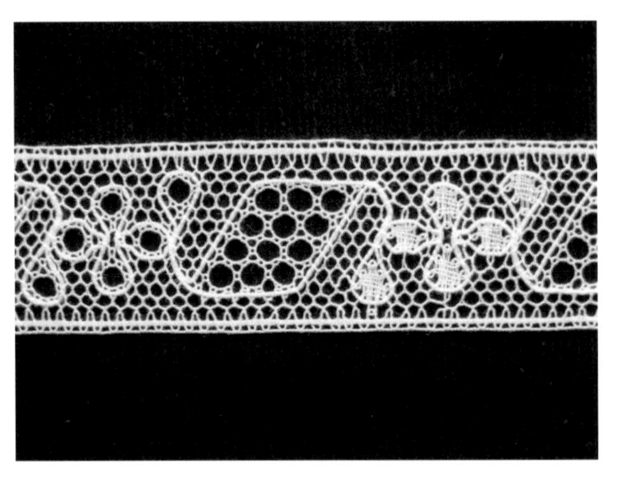

Worked by Christine Wood

Thread:	100/2 Egyptian Cotton DMC Cotton Perle No 12
Bobbins:	20 pairs
Gimp:	1 pair
Oval shapes:	Either honeycomb or cloth stitch
Diamonds:	Honeycomb.
Ground:	Net ground.
Footside:	2 pairs of passives worked in cloth stitch with a catch stitch on the inside edge.

Net ground *= half stitch + 2 twists pinned between the twisted pairs.*

Catch stitch *= pin is placed to the right of the twisted pairs instead of between them.*

MJ10

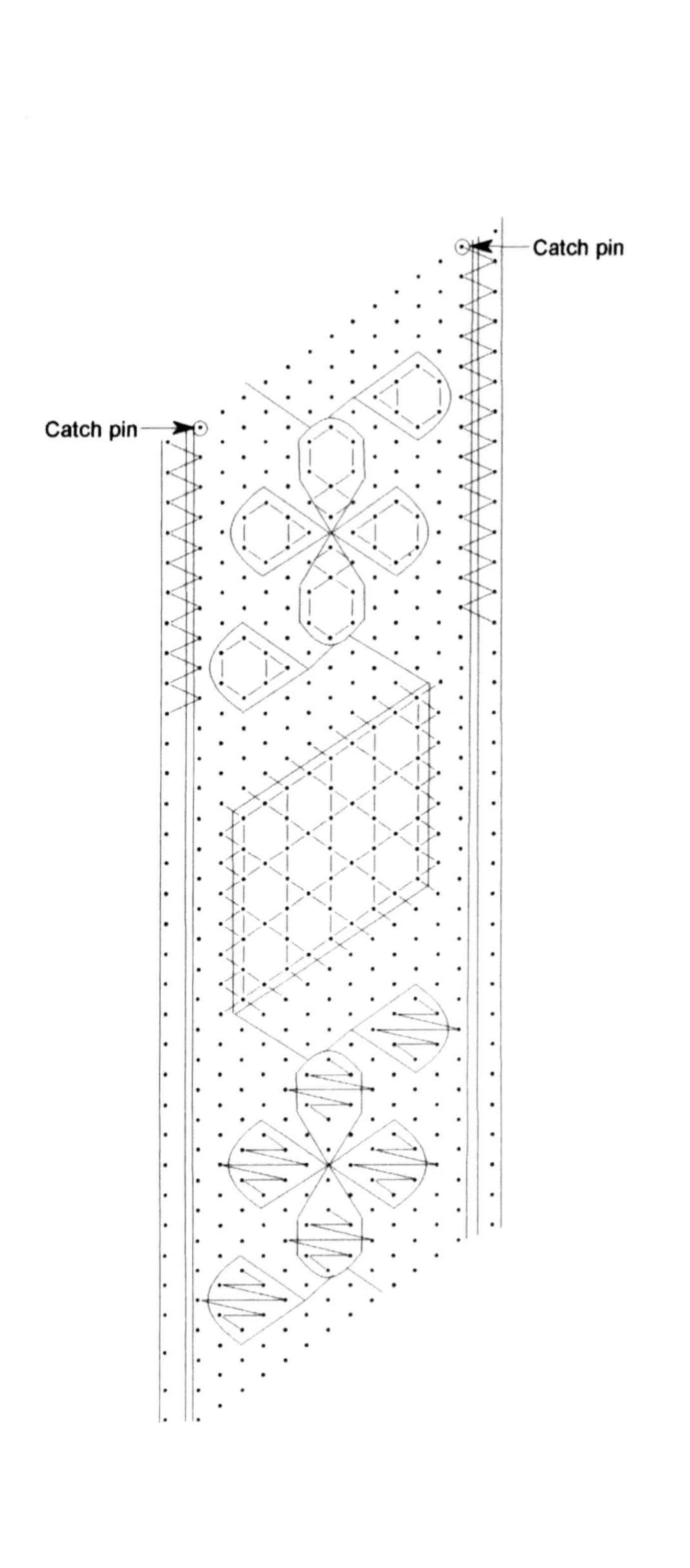

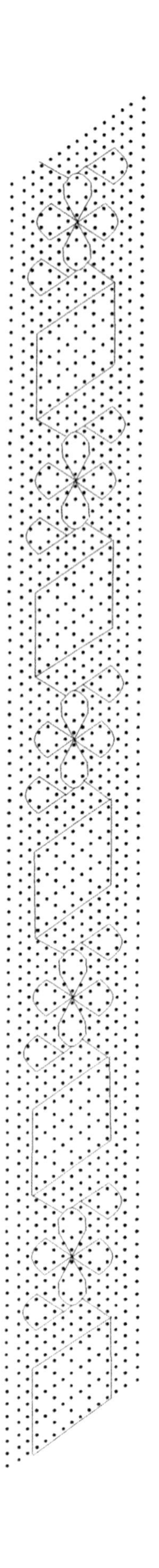

MJ11

Once again there was no worked lace sample for this design although the pricking did have some marks suggesting gimp lines. It is a beautiful fine lace edging with a busy gimp. Whilst the pattern appears similar to both Lille and Bucks Point it closely resembles Tønder lace pattern No 34 in 'Tulekantpatronen' by Henk Hardeman (1982).

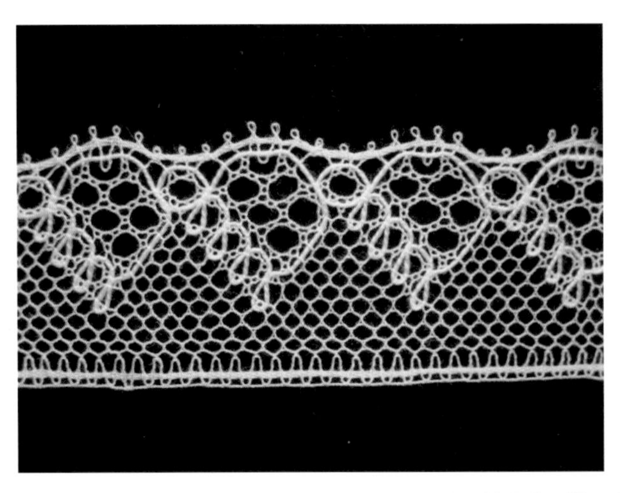

Worked by Christine Wood

Thread:	100/2 Egyptian Cotton DMC Cotton Perle No 12
Bobbins:	22 pairs
Gimp:	1 pair
Headside:	2 pairs worked in cloth stitch + a picot.
Inside gimps:	Honeycomb.
Ground:	Net ground.
Footside:	2 pairs of passives worked in cloth stitch with a catch stitch on the inside edge.

Net ground *= half stitch + 2 twists pinned between the twisted pairs.*

Catch stitch *= pin is placed to the right of the twisted pairs instead of between them.*

NOTE: *For clarity, gimps are marked in blue on this technical drawing.*

MJ11

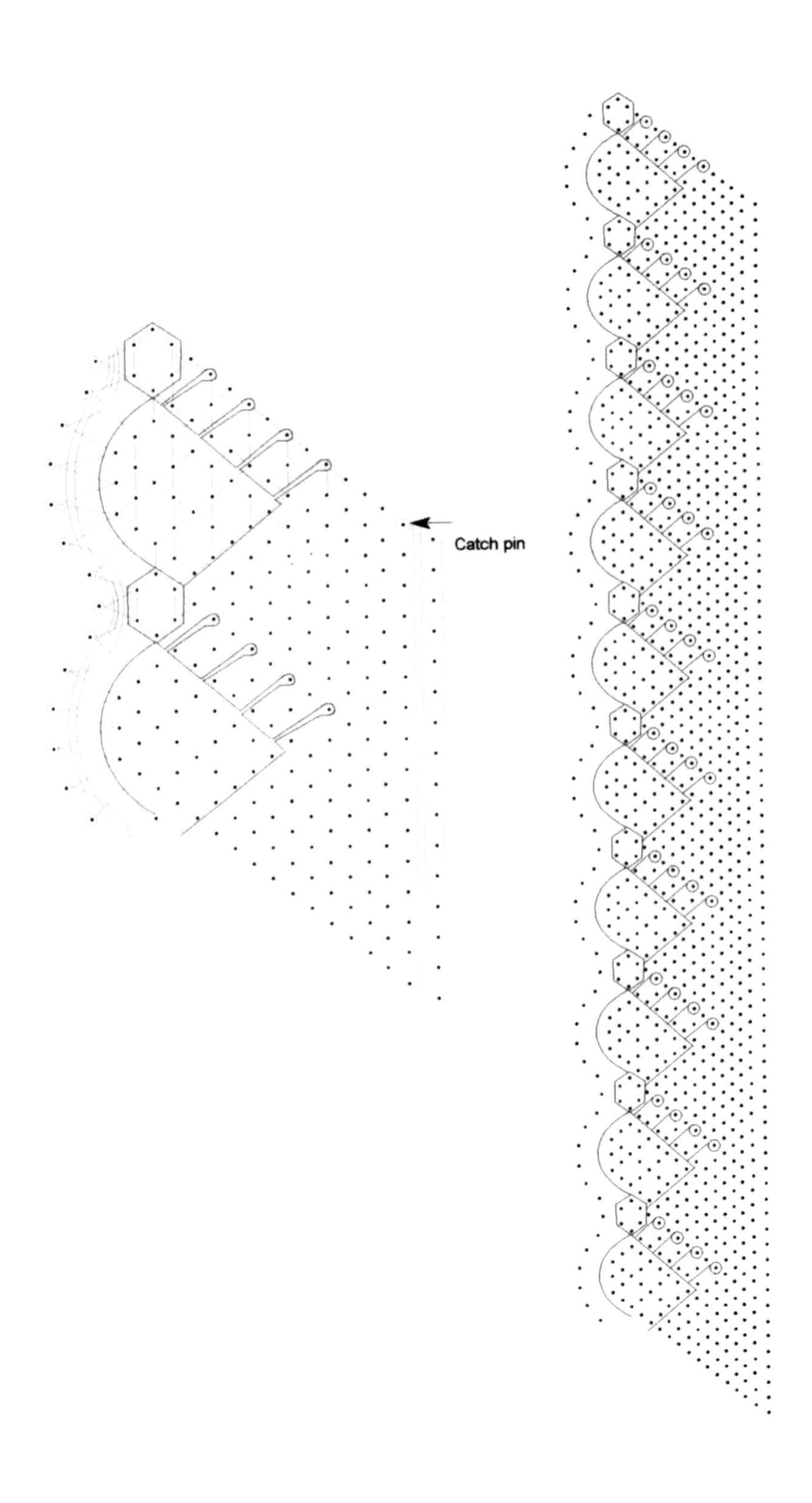

MJ12

Only a pricking showing light gimp marks was found for this broad, fine lace edging. It is almost identical to No 456 in the Palliser Collection housed at the Royal Albert Museum in Exeter.

Worked by Christine Wood

Thread:	100/2 Egyptian Cotton DMC Cotton Perle No 12
Bobbins:	30 pairs
Gimp:	1 pair
Headside:	2 pairs worked in cloth stitch + a picot.
Inside gimps:	Honeycomb.
Diamonds:	Cloth stitch with 2 twists on adjoining bars.
Ground:	Net ground.
Footside:	2 pairs of passives worked in cloth stitch with a catch stitch on the inside edge.

Net ground *= half stitch + 2 twists pinned between the twisted pairs.*

Catch stitch *= pin is placed to the right of the twisted pairs instead of between them.*

MJ12

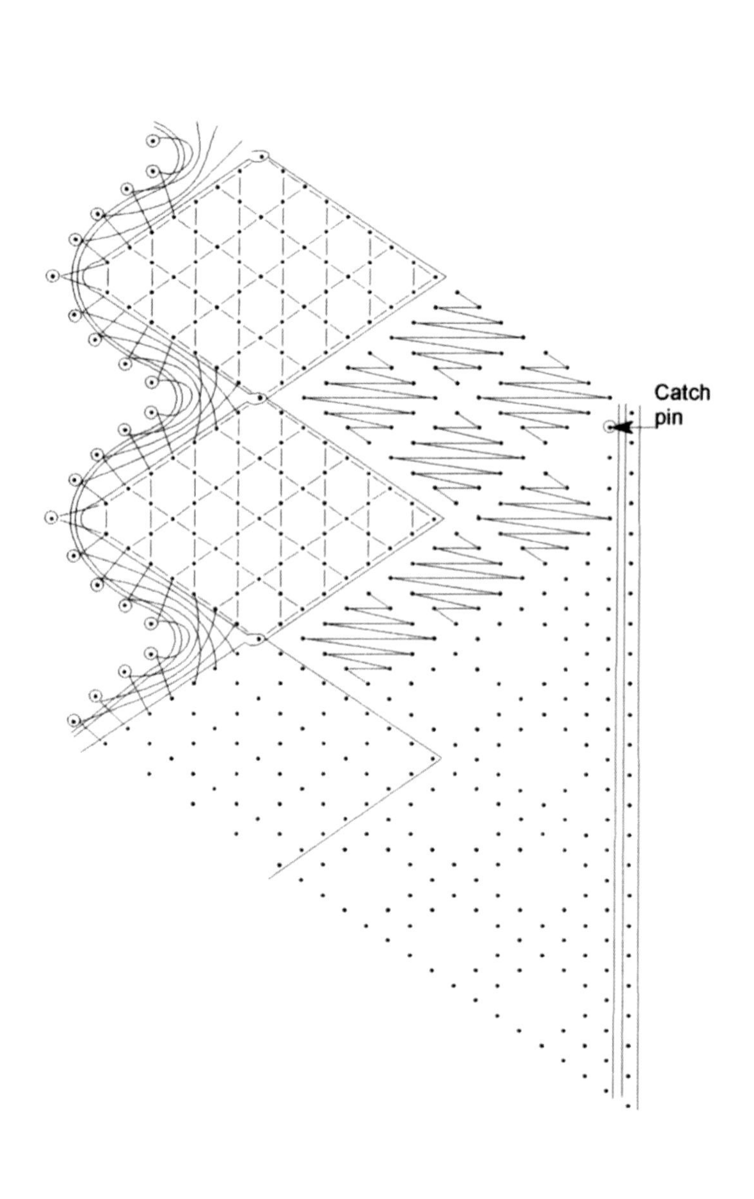

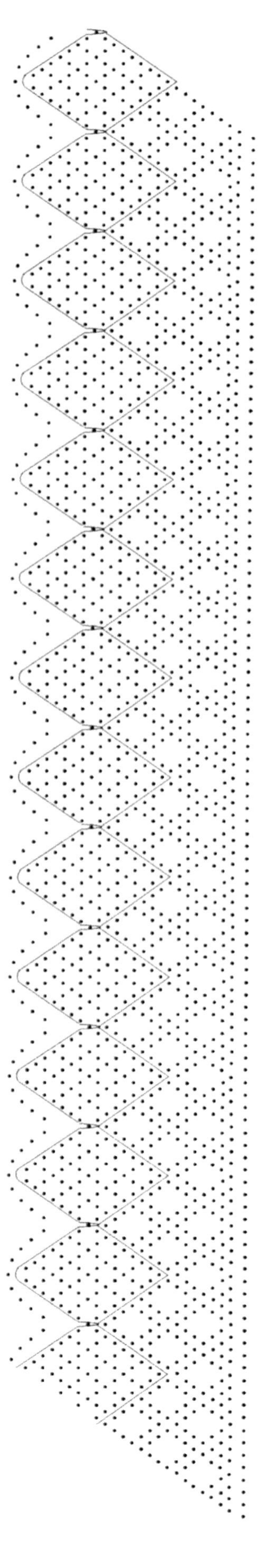

MJ13

A simple, narrow Bedfordshire edging worked from a pricking that was irregularly marked with a suggested design.

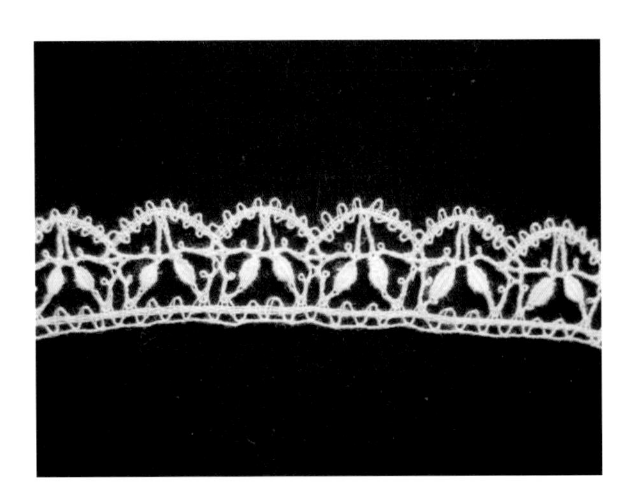

Thread:	70/2 Egyptian Cotton
Bobbins:	11 pairs
Headside:	2 pairs worked in cloth stitch with 3 twists round the pins. See diagram A on the technical drawing which shows how to change pairs when the plait meets the trail with no twists round the pin.
Inner design:	Plaits with picots and leaves.
Footside:	3 twists, work through 2 passive pairs in cloth stitch + 3 twists on worker, cloth stitch through the edge pair and twist both pairs 3 times. Work back through the 2 passive pairs in cloth stitch and twist the worker 3 times.

MJ13

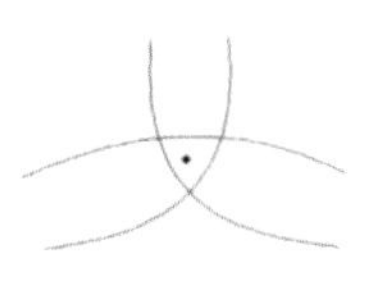

Diagram A

Working direction

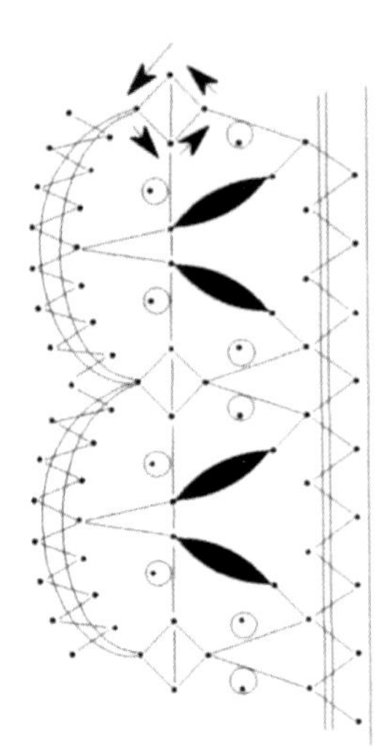

MJ14

This very attractive Bedfordshire pattern was worked in accordance with some scant directions marked on the original pricking.

Worked by Mary Ellis

Thread:	70/2 Egyptian Cotton
Bobbins:	+/- 31 pairs
Picots:	5 twists.
Trellis:	3 twists, cloth, 3 twists.
Trails:	3 pairs with 3 twists each end.
Footside:	3 twists, work through 3 passive pairs in cloth stitch + 3 twists on worker, cloth stitch through edge pair and twist both pairs 3 times. Work back through the 3 passive pairs in cloth stitch and twist the worker 3 times. A tally joins the trail to the footside.

MJ14

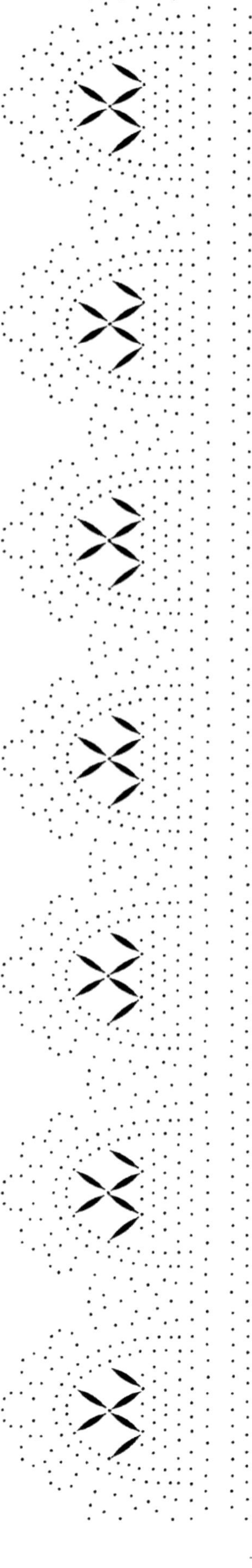

MJ15

A particularly inaccurate but exceptionally well used pricking was found for this very pretty and rather uncommon shell pattern. It is not unlike a design found in the lace collection at Luton Museum which was used as a picture guide when re-working this pattern.

Thread:	70/2 Egyptian Cotton DMC Cotton Perle No 12
Bobbins:	19 pairs
Gimp:	7 bobbins
Headside:	2 pairs worked in cloth stitch + a picot. The gimp outlining the top of the shell has 1 passive pair worked in cloth stitch running underneath it and the worker is twisted either side of the gimp.
Trails in shell:	1 pair worked in cloth stitch running above the gimp with twists between them.
Triangles:	Honeycomb.
Ground:	Half stitch, pin, half stitch and an extra twist.
Footside:	1 passive pair worked in double stitch and an extra twist on the worker. The edge stitch is worked in double stitch with an extra twist on the worker and 2 extra twists on outside edge pair. Work double stitch back through the passive pair with an extra twist on both pairs.

Twist twice before and after passing through the gimp whichever direction you are working.
When beginning the shell pass the inner gimps down to enter their respective trails before bringing the main outlining gimp up.
To end the shell take the main outlining gimp back down to the footside before passing the inner gimps up to the headside.
Both gimps travel across the bottom of the honeycomb diamond between the shells.

Double stitch *= Cloth stitch +1 twist on both pairs*

NOTE: *For clarity, gimps are marked in blue on this technical drawing.*

MJ15

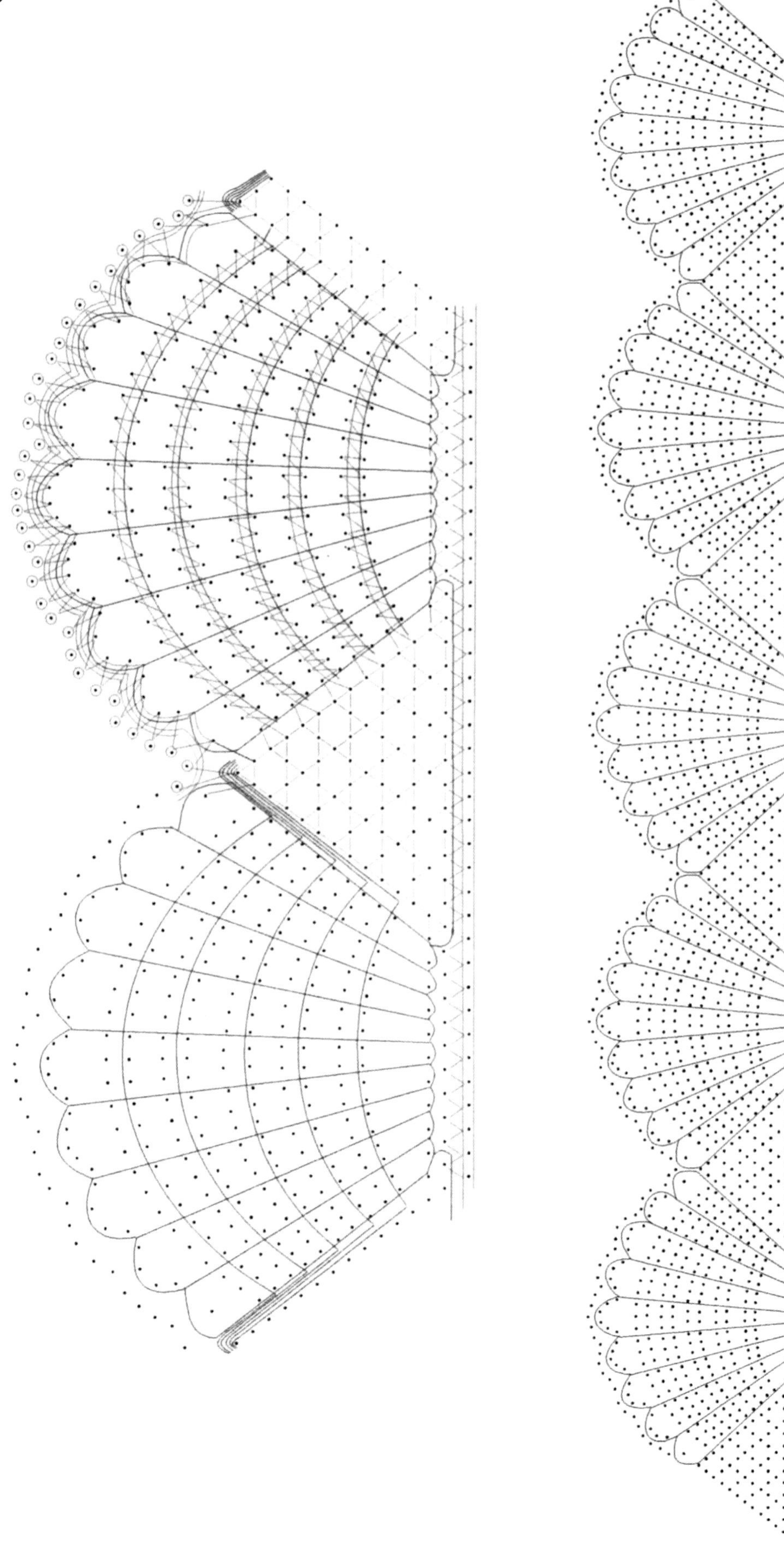

MJ16

Unfortunately there was no sample for this design only a pricking with some extremely irregular and faint marks on it. It is a very beautiful Bedfordshire design which has been reproduced with little alteration other than straightening it up here and there. Evelyn Burnell suggested that the different trails in this complex pattern should be clearly identified to assist the lacemaker. They have been grouped and coloured on the technical drawing to this end.

Worked by Evelyn Burnell

Thread:	80 Egyptian cotton
Bobbins:	+/- 60 pairs
Trails:	Cloth stitch through 2 or 3 pairs of passives. Each group of trails is identified by a different colour on the technical drawing.
Fillings:	Plaits, plaits + picots, tallies, leaves, Leaves made into flowers with half stitch centres.
Footside:	3 twists, work through 2 passive pairs in cloth stitch + 3 twists on worker, cloth stitch through edge pair and twist both pairs 3 times. Work back through the 3 passive pairs in cloth stitch and twist the worker 3 times.

The pattern can either be worked as has been suggested here or you may prefer to work your own interpretation of the design.

MJ16

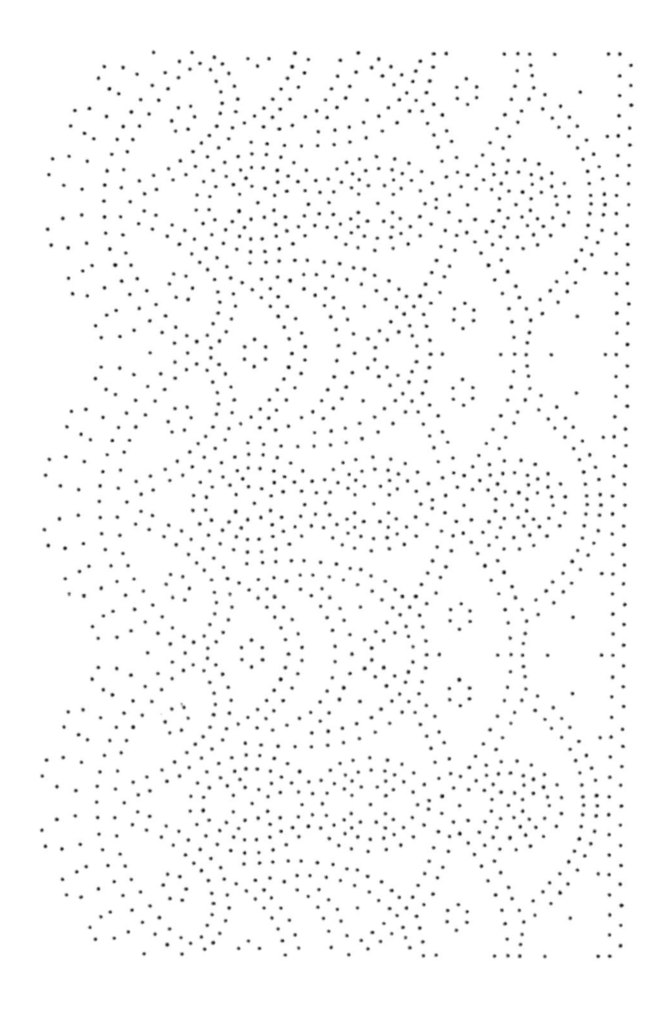

HM1

This appealing pattern was drafted from an old piece of lace which had been donated from an unknown source to the Harrogate Museums and Arts lace collection. As explained at the beginning of this chapter it closely resembles Hamilton lace and the diamonds and bars are worked exactly as described in an encyclopaedia which details the techniques on how to make Ripon lace.

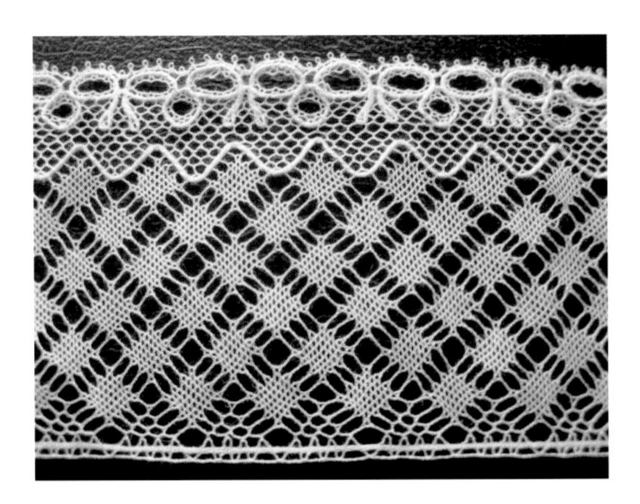

Thread:	100/2 Egyptian Cotton DMC Cotton Perle No 8
Bobbins:	43 pairs
Gimp:	1 pair + 1 single bobbin
Headside:	1 pair worked in cloth stitch + a picot
Edge design:	Honeycomb rings with 'fingers' worked into the net ground all outlined by the gimps.
Diamonds:	Half stitch with 3 twists on adjoining bars.
Ground:	Net ground
Footside:	2 pairs of passives worked in cloth stitch with a catch stitch on the inside edge.

Net ground *= half stitch + 2 twists pinned between the twisted pairs.*

Catch stitch *= pin is placed to the right of the twisted pairs instead of between them.*

NOTE: Because the headside is so irregular there are only 2 complete pattern repeats on the pricking printed here.

HM1

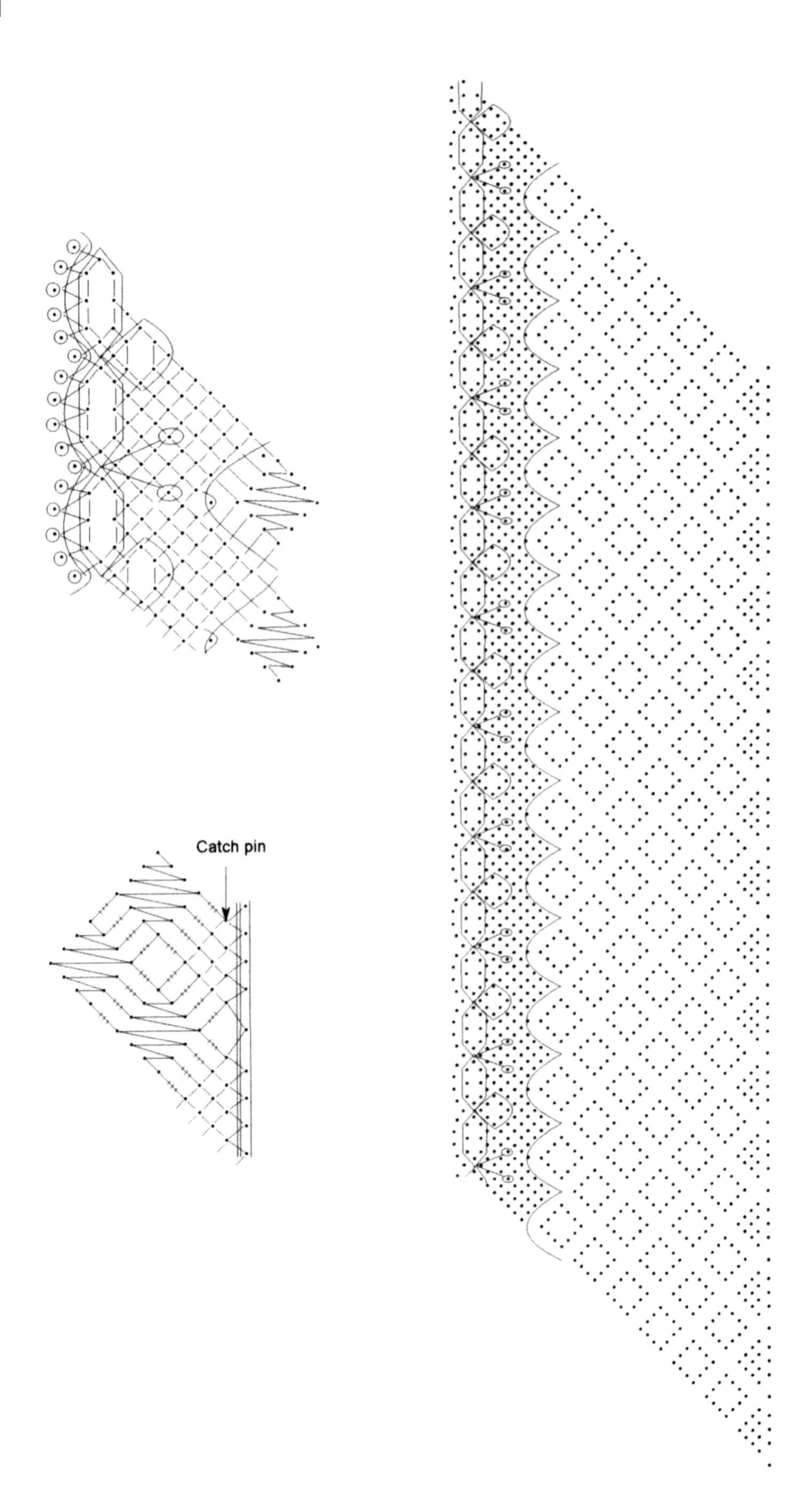

HM2

This second pattern from Harrogate Museums and Arts has been redrafted from a piece of lace in the Kent Collection. At first glance it looks like it might be worked in a course linen thread but it is in fact a delicate, fine cotton and gimp insertion. The unusual Rose Ground filling together with the crisp geometric shapes make it an attractive and flexible design.

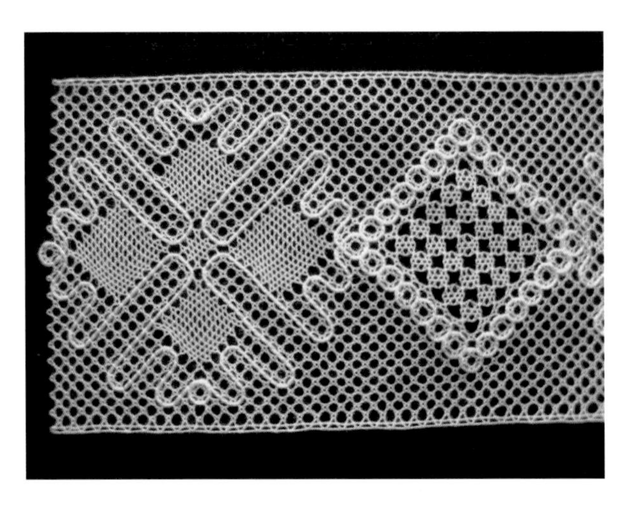

Worked by Christine Wood

Thread:	70/2 Egyptian Cotton DMC Cotton Perle No 8
Bobbins:	46 pairs
Gimp:	2 pairs
Rings:	Half stitch, pin, half stitch
Diamond filling:	Rose ground, see diagram.
Ground:	Half stitch, pin, half stitch + 1 twist.
Cross:	The diamond shape is worked in half stitch with 'spurs' outlined by the gimp in the ground.
Footside:	1 passive pair worked in double stitch with an extra twist on the worker. The edge stitch is worked in double stitch with an extra twist on the worker and 2 extra twists on outside edge pair. Work double stitch back through the passive pair with an extra twist on both pairs.

***Double stitch** = Cloth stitch +1 twist on both pairs*

HM2

Rose Ground filling in diamond.

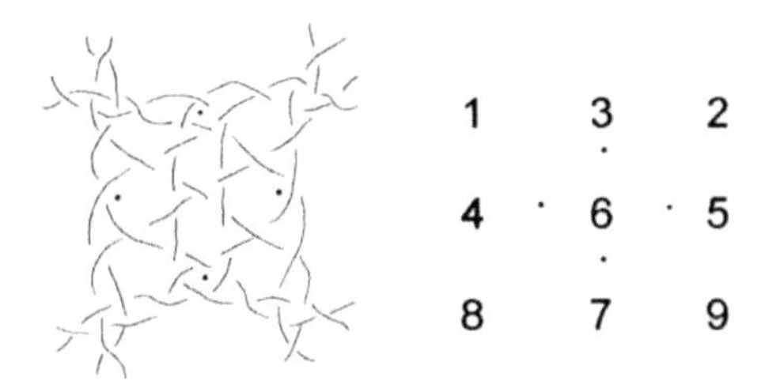

1 + 2	Cloth stitch +1 twist
3	Half stitch, pin, half stitch
4 + 5	Half stitch, pin
6	With middle 2 pairs from pins at 4 + 5 work a half stitch
4 + 5	Half stitch to cover pin
7	Half stitch, pin, half stitch
8 + 9	Cloth stitch +1 twist

Ripon Horn - Binche

The Ripon Horn that appears on the cover of this book is worked in Binche Lace. There is no evidence to suggest that Binche lace was ever worked in Ripon although Harker's crochet pattern, which can be seen on the inside cover, does bring to mind the same Paris Ground.

A pricking and detailed technical drawing has been included to assist the lacemaker when working this pattern.

Designed by Mary Moseley with the help of Anne-Marie Verbeke Billiet

Thread:	120/2 Egyptian Cotton for the small pricking Cotton a Broder No 25 or 80/2 Egyptian Cotton for the large pricking Cotton a Broder No 20
Bobbins:	+/- 124 pairs
Gimp:	+/- 12 bobbins
Ground:	Double stitch Paris ground. Binche snowflakes worked in both cloth and half stitch.
Ribbons:	Cloth with half stitch knot and where they are wrapped round the horn.
Horn:	Half stitch ovals with the rest of the shapes that represent the outside of the horn worked in cloth stitch.

Refer to the technical drawing for more detailed instructions.

Ripon Horn

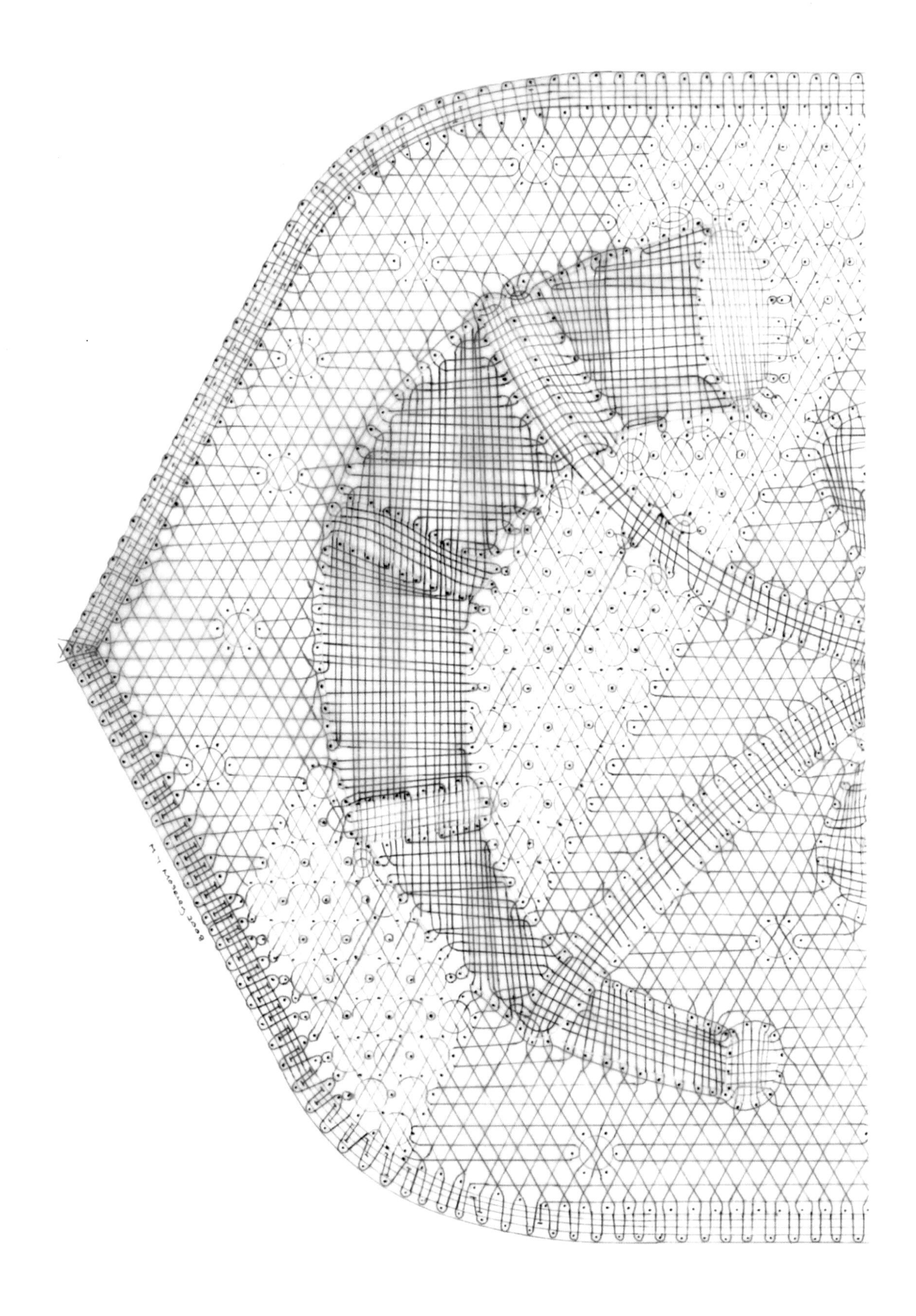